# In Brigid's Footsteps

## The Return of the Divine Feminine

Linda W. McFadden

CHIRON PUBLICATIONS • ASHEVILLE, NORTH CAROLINA

www.ChironPublications.com

Interior and cover design by Danijela Mijailovic
Printed primarily in the United States of America.

"Hymn to Sant Ffraid" by Ruth Bidgood is © Ruth Bidgood, 2006. Published by Canterbury Press. Used by permission. rights@hymnsam.co.uk

"On St. Brigid's Day" from "Crossings" from OPENED GROUND: SELECTED POEMS 1966-1996 by Seamus Heaney. Copyright © 1998 by Seamus Heaney. Reprinted by permission of Farrar, Straus and Giroux. All Rights Reserved.

ISBN  978-1-63051-956-8 paperback
ISBN  978-1-63051-957-5 hardcover
ISBN  978-1-63051-958-2 electronic
ISBN  978-1-63051-959-9 limited edition paperback

Library of Congress Cataloging-in-Publication Data Pending

I am the thought that lives in the light.
I live in everyone, and I delve into them all . . .
I move in every creature. . . .
I am the invisible one in all beings . . .
I am a voice speaking softly . . .
I am the real voice, the voice from the invisible thought . . .
It is a mystery . . . I cry out in everyone . . .
I hid myself within everyone and revealed myself within
them,
and every mind seeking me longs for me . . .
I am she who brought forth everything . . .
I am the image of the invisible spirit . . .
The mother, the light . . . the virgin . . . the womb and
the voice.

> *The Nag Hammadi Library*, ca. 4th century C.E.

The exclusion of the feminine energy in our naming and understanding of the divine is reflected in a corresponding absence and valuing of feminine energy in all aspects of life in western society. The devaluing and exclusion of feminine energy over the past centuries has created a distorted story about life that has resulted in a world whose shape and vibration creates disharmony.

> Dolores Whelan

God used to rage at the Israelites for frequenting sacred groves. I wish I could find one.

> Annie Dillard, *Teaching a Stone to Talk*

# Dedication

To Philip

# Acknowledgements

Much of the credit for the inspiration of this book goes to John Philip Newell for opening my eyes to the realms of Celtic Christianity and to Jerry Wright for his lucid tutelage and mentoring in Jungian psychology. Inspiration has also come from the spirit-charged island of Iona itself, with special thanks to Rose Wilkerson for leading that first visit to the Well of Eternal Youth. I am indebted to fellow pilgrims, to the congregations I have served, and the students in my writing classes for all I have learned from them throughout many years. Bouquets of gratitude for the invaluable support that brought this book from conception to birth go to Barbara Kovaz for listening to my ideas, to my Haden Institute spiritual direction alumni gang for their encouragement, to Jennifer Fitzgerald and the staff of Chiron Publications for making the publication process so agreeable, and most especially to my husband, Philip Wiehe, my number one advocate, champion, and cheerleader throughout this process.

# Table of Contents

# Introduction

Once in Ireland long ago, according to legend, the family of a minor chieftain arranged a suitable match for their daughter who had reached marriageable age. The girl's name was Brigid. The family was pleased with the match and the bride price it would bring, but Brigid had always been stubborn and willful, and now the ungrateful girl refused to get married. She had some daft notion that instead of having a husband and family like any normal young woman, she wanted to marry Jesus Christ. In the end, her obstinacy won out. She not only found a way to be consecrated as a nun, but she also founded a double monastery and became its abbess, becoming in time one of the most powerful and influential women in Ireland. She became known as St. Brigid of Kildare.

One account of the saint's life discloses the strength of Brigid's determination to follow her calling. After Brigid had finally persuaded her family that she would not marry, she set off with seven other young women who shared a desire to take the veil in search of a bishop to consecrate them as Brides of Christ. Their journey was far from easy, for in those days, Ireland had few roadways, no road maps, and certainly no vocational guidebooks whatever for young women who wanted to become nuns. Nevertheless, Brigid and her companions made their way to the place where they had heard Bishop Mel was living, a small religious house on the side of Cróchán, an island of high ground surrounded on all sides by boglands. The sisters there greeted them regretfully with the news that the bishop was away visiting the churches in another area. Brigid and her companions then asked a young man who was studying with Bishop Mel if he would lead them to the bishop, but the youth declined, saying that "the way is trackless, with marshes, deserts, bogs and pools." Brigid was undeterred by the roughness of the unmarked terrain. She and her companions simply headed off in the direction the student had pointed. As the young man watched the women forging ahead across the marshes, "he could see afterwards a straight bridge there" (*Bethu Brigte*, §17).

The bridge formed by Brigid's footsteps as she strode into unmarked terrain has become for me an image of the energy of the Divine Feminine leading our masculine-leaning culture forward through these unsettled times. I began writing this book with the intention of introducing Brigid to readers who share an interest in Jungian psychology, Celtic spirituality, mythology, and the Divine Feminine. When I first encountered Brigid during a pilgrimage to Iona, her initial appeal for me was that she manifested many qualities of the Divine Feminine that are absent in Western mythology and mainstream culture. Moreover, as she has shape-shifted throughout centuries, she has embodied the Divine Feminine in a variety of cultural circumstances.

Questions arose as I pursued Brigid. It seemed that I could not write about the archetypal Brigid without considering both the context in which she has flourished and the larger environment in which the feminine has not thrived. What made Celtic culture especially hospitable to the Divine Feminine? And what made Western civilization as a whole inimical to the feminine? Brigid, the patroness of inspiration herself, seemed to raise further speculations. What if the feminine energies of fertility, nurturance, inspiration, wisdom, and connectivity were blended with the masculine forms of power esteemed by Western civilization? In a time when we are due for what Jung called a "changing of the gods," or new constellation of archetypes that will lead us into the next stages of the evolution of consciousness, might the emerging mythology portray the universe as a collaboration of feminine and masculine energies?

In the Western world, even atheists "know" that God is masculine. Yet, this assumption handed down from generation to generation is by no means a universal perception. The alternative construct that the universe is a dynamic collaboration of masculine and feminine energies is upheld by the discoveries of modern quantum physics as well as by ancient Eastern spiritual traditions. The ancient Taoist *taijitu* symbol depicting the cosmic dance of *yang* and *yin* that comprises the universe might have been custom designed to illustrate physicist Fritjof Capra's description of the universe as "a continuous dance of energy."[1] This cosmic dance of Yang and Yin forms the basis of the *I Ching*, the 3,000-year-old system of cosmic archetypes whose enigmatic oracles Jung found to be a valuable balance to linear Western modes of thought. The synergy of masculine and feminine energies is expressed in Hinduism as the dance of Shiva, the Cosmic Dancer, and Shakti, the Divine Mother, without which nothing in the universe exists, as a Sanskrit hymn attests: "If Shiva is united with Shakti, he is able to create. If he is not, he is incapable even of stirring." Even the Hebrew Scriptures include intimations of the primal partnership of masculine and feminine energies in such passages as the eighth chapter of Proverbs, in which Sophia, or Divine Wisdom, reminisces about the joyful partnership she enjoyed with YHWH in creating the world.

This vibrant partnership has not found a place in predominant Western mythology. The myths available to us simply don't work very well in the 21st century as a means to orient ourselves in the universe because they represent the spiritual wisdom of times long past. As Joseph Campbell has put it:

> Surely it is folly to preach to children who will be riding rockets to the moon a morality and cosmology based on concepts of the Good Society and of man's place in nature that were coined before the harnessing of the horse! And the world is now too small, and men's stake in sanity too great, for any of those old games of Chosen Folk (whether of Jehovah, Allah, Wotan, Manu, or the Devil) by which tribesmen were sustained against their enemies in the days when the serpent still could talk.[2]

The view of reality in which a masculine deity reigns over all, giving his divine sanction to hierarchical social arrangements and denigrating the feminine, has produced a profoundly unbalanced civilization that allows science and technology to reach unparalleled heights of achievement yet leaves human spirits in a desiccated, impoverished condition. Yet, the very notion that there could be new "gods" is blasphemy to many because the old mythology is enshrined within Western religions as divinely revealed Truth. The emergence of many types of religious fundamentalism represents determined attempts to hang on to the old ideas of Ultimate Reality. Even so, the emergence of new archetypes is inevitable. New mythology is not something we decide to make happen but something that we need to *allow* to happen.

This book that Brigid inspired has grown to include an exploration of the Divine Feminine in the evolution of consciousness. Part I focuses on Brigid as an avatar of the Divine Feminine, from her origins as a Mother Goddess to Iron Age cultural goddess to Christian saint. Part II investigates three mysteries of Brigid's context: how the Goddess came to be suppressed in Western culture; why Celtic culture sustained an understanding of dynamic feminine energy; and how Irish monks saved Celtic mythology from oblivion. Part III speculates on how the return of the Divine Feminine in our time may affect the renewal of mythology and the evolution of consciousness.

My deepest wish is that the stories and ideas in this book that Brigid inspired may ignite your own dreams and visions of a more fully conscious way of life in our mysterious and dynamic universe.

# PART ONE
# Goddess Quest

# Chapter One
# Finding Brigid

With all the Irish a goddess was called *Brigit.*
*Sanas Cormaic*, 9th century

On a rare sunny afternoon in Iona, six exuberant pilgrims toiled up the rugged slope of Dun I, the highest point on the tiny Hebridean island. From the moment we rolled our wheelie bags down the ramp of the little ferry that transported us across the narrow strait from the Isle of Mull, every aspect of Iona had filled us with childish delight: the wee village, the ancient stones of the ruined Nunnery and the Abbey, the sheep and cattle grazing in verdant fields, the sea-polished varicolored rocks, the wild geese on the wing. This afternoon, we were intent on finding the Well of Eternal Youth we had heard was up on top of Dun I. We arrived at the summit, panting and giddy with excitement, after helping each other up the steep path, over boulders, boggy dips, and sheep droppings. What greeted us at the summit took our breaths away—views of endless expanses of sea and sky surrounding the Lilliputian island spread beneath us. We had not dreamed that our curiosity about a holy well would lead to being magically suspended in the Celtic trinity of earth, sea and sky.

The Well of Eternal Youth turned out to be a picturesque triangular pool set between massive boulders and surrounded by a fringe of reeds. As we celebrated our arrival by snapping photos, sprawling in the grass, or playfully "baptizing" each other, something in the reeds snagged my eye. Closer investigation revealed it to be a peculiar little lopsided cross no bigger than the palm of my hand, woven from the green reeds, a St. Brigid's Cross. It must have been a spontaneous votive offering woven on the spot by an anonymous pilgrim. It seemed a prayer of gratitude and praise for this numinous place where earth, sea, and sky met. No spoken prayer could have been a more eloquent tribute to the presence of the Holy in that place.

Painted on a wall just inside the doors of Iona Abbey is a Celtic saying: "Heaven and Earth are only three feet apart, but in thin places, the distance is even smaller." In the nature-centered Celtic world, rivers, springs, and wells like this one were thin places, for they were apertures into the sacred body of the Goddess. This well was just such a sacred place, and the little Brigid's cross I found there propelled me into a numinous realm. Suddenly, it became clear that the Celtic Christianity of Iona had been rocked in the arms of the Goddess.

## Following Brigid

About all I knew about St. Brigid of Kildare back then was that she was part of Ireland's trinity of national saints, along with St. Patrick and St. Columba. I soon learned that the iconic St. Brigid shares a name and many attributes with a Celtic goddess. The goddess has been known variously as Brigit, Brighid, Brighidh, Bride, Brid, Bridget, Breeshy, Brigindo, Brigitte, or Ffraid (in Welsh). In Haiti, where she

10

was transplanted by colonial emigrants from Celtic countries, she even crops up as a Voodoo goddess called Maman Brigitte. The statement in a medieval encyclopedia that "with all the Irish a goddess was called Brigit" implies that in a goddess-rich Celtic mythology, Brigid was a kind of "uber goddess."

"Brigid" or "Bride" can also refer to the saintly Brigid of Kildare, who is venerated as the mother of the Irish Church. Saint and goddess share many attributes, but as to just how they are related, you can take your pick of theories. One school of thought sees St. Brigid of Kildare as evidence that the Irish Church took advantage of the popularity of a pagan goddess to promote Christianity. There are also "goddess deniers" who say that no pre-Christian Brigid ever existed; they believe that the goddess was a fiction created retrospectively from the attributes of the saint. Still another theory of origin links St. Brigid with Druidism. According to this school of thought, the Druid temple at Kildare ("Cill Dara" or "Church of the Oak Tree") had a chief priestess called "The Brigid." When The Brigid converted to Christianity and founded a double monastery on the site, she brought along the temple's sacred fire, along with some of her sister priestesses to tend it. For my money, the best characterization of Brigid is Sir James Frazer's one-liner. He calls Brigid "an old heathen goddess of fertility, disguised in a threadbare Christian cloak."

If you detect a certain imprecision in these characterizations, you are right. Early in my pursuit of Brigid, I learned that information about her origins is rather short on facts and long on speculation. My quest to know Brigid and the world from which she emerged began with books and websites, but her footsteps soon led me to travels far beyond my desk. Finding Brigid meant opening myself to history as well as to places where the Divine Feminine had left her mark. I visited archaeological sites in Spanish Galicia to see how ancient Celts lived, sought out holy wells in Ireland and Glastonbury, and found my way to the church in Portugal where St. Brigid's skull reposes in an ornate golden reliquary and scenes from her life are depicted in beautiful blue and white tiles.

The only hints of a goddess named Brig or Brigid prior to the early Middle Ages when literacy was introduced to Ireland are linguistic, but tracing Brigid's roots through linguistic clues is complicated by the many variations of her name. In Irish, her name is written *Brighid* or *Bríd,* pronounced with a hard "g" as "Brigg-id." In Scots Gaelic, she is *Brighde* or *Bríde*. In modern Gaelic, her name is spelled "Brighid" and pronounced "Bree-id," with the "g" being silent. In this book, I have opted to use the form "Brigid" (pronounced "Bridjit") rather than attempt a Gaelic pronunciation that might be a stumbling block for Anglophone readers. Variant spellings of her name are preserved in quoted sources throughout the text.

*Brig,* the Celtic word from which Brigid's name stems, meant "High One" or "Exalted One." Originally it was an epithet of the mother goddess. The Celts, who revered sound as a sacred power, habitually addressed deities by epithets because they wanted to avoid profaning sacred names by pronouncing them aloud. The epithet *brig* eventually became the name of a mother goddess called Brigid.

The main reason that evidence of Brigid's origins is so scarce is that the Celts declined to adopt literacy, preferring to transmit their culture orally. Some might consider refusal to learn to read and write as a sign of ignorance or sheer pigheadedness, but the Celts' abstention from literacy was spiritually motivated. Moreover, their determination to remain an oral culture may paradoxically have been a factor in maintaining the central role of the Divine Feminine in Celtic mythology, a topic I will discuss in Chapter 7. The Celts maintained an extensive body of knowledge, including history, genealogy, law, natural science, stories, and poetry entirely by oral transmission, but since they never committed any of it to writing, most of that content is lost to us. What we do know about them comes entirely through eyes of outsiders, including Greek and Roman writers and the Irish Christian monks who transcribed some of the oral material. From the Classical writers we hear much of the Celts as invaders and warriors, with an occasional grudging word of praise for their bravery. Classical writings also testify to the astounding breadth of knowledge held by the Druids who were the priests, teachers, and philosophers of the Celts, but they tell us little about their religion, and about Brigid, nothing at all.

Ironically, written references to a goddess called Brigid come entirely from the pens of medieval Irish monks who transcribed the oral Celtic mythology. These monastic scribes also produced several accounts of the miraculous life of St. Brigid of Kildare. Even after these divergent versions of Brigid the goddess and Brigid the saint began to appear in the pages of Irish literature, another version of Brigid evolved through the richly imagined oral folklore and popular religion that entwined attributes of the ancient goddess with those of the saint. The role the monastic scribes played in the transmission of Brigid is the subject of Chapter 8.

# Chapter Two
# The Irish Goddess

Ireland *is* the goddess. She is every field still fertile a thousand years after its first cultivation. She is every river that still floods with salmon despite millennia of fishing. She is the dancing pattern of the seasons, the fecundity of sheep and cattle, the messages written in the migratory flight of birds. She is the sun's heat stored deep in the dark bogs. She is the refreshment of pure water and of golden ale. She is living nature and she has never been forgotten in Ireland.

Patricia Monaghan

It is pointless to search for Irish goddesses, because once you are on Irish soil, you are already immersed in the Feminine. The fertile earth of Ireland is the body of the Mother, the flowing waters of springs and rivers are entrances to her womb, and the local mountains are her breasts.

The first Gaels who stepped onto Ireland's shore, the Milesians, were greeted by three sister goddesses who represented the land—Fodla, Banba, and Eriu. Each goddess in turn asked the new colonists to name the island in her honor. Ultimately, the Milesians named the land "Eire" or

"Erin" in honor of Eriu, but in the end, all three goddesses assisted the Milesians in their quest to possess the island. Triple goddesses in Celtic mythology always indicate the presence of great power—Divine Feminine power multiplied by the sacred number three. Brigid herself was sometimes depicted as a trinity of sister goddesses—Brigid the Poet, Brigid the Physician, and Brigid the Smith. The Milesians were greeted by the Divine Feminine energy that is inextricable from the land of Ireland.

The identification of natural features of the land with the Mother's body is still reflected in modern maps. One example is the use of the word "paps," an archaic term for "breasts," applied to certain conical hills and mountains, such as the "Paps of Jura" in the Hebrides and the "Paps of the Mórrígan" in the Boyne Valley. The "Paps of Anu" in County Kerry literally translates as the "Breasts of the Mother Goddess" (Anu). Besides their suggestive conical shape, the likeness of the Paps of Anu to breasts is enhanced by prehistoric stone cairns constructed at the top of each peak that have the appearance of nipples. Archaeological investigation of the cairns has revealed that the Paps of Anu have been an important ritual site since the Bronze Age, well before the Celtic occupation of Ireland.

We have no way of knowing how far back in time Irish oral mythology goes, but scholars have established that the oldest fragments go back to a time when worship still centered on a Mother Goddess. The ninth-century Irish dictionary *Sanas Cormaic* ("Cormac's Glossary") says that the mother of the Irish gods was called "Anu" or "Danu," yet curiously, Irish mythology seldom refers to the Mother Goddess by name. The form "Danu" is conjectured from the tribal name *Tuatha Dé Danann* ("Tribes of the Goddess Danu"), the semidivine ancestral spirits, sometimes rendered simply as *Tuatha Dé* ("Tribes of the Goddess"). The name "Danu," which means "to flow," appears throughout Indo-European cultures in connection with water, especially in the names of rivers. Her name is given to the Danube, the Dneiper, and the Don in Europe. She appears in the Rigveda as the embodiment of the primordial waters and mother of the serpent Vritra. In Balinese Hinduism, which is called "the belief system of the waters," she is revered as a water goddess.

The epithet "Brig" or "Exalted One" for the Mother Goddess appears to have evolved into a goddess called Brigid who was conflated with Anu/Danu in the myths. As a Mother Goddess, Brigid was associated with fundamental responsibility for fertility, the production of milk, and the well-being of animals. She guarded the hearth fire at the center of the home and watched over the two thresholds of life, birth and death. Brigid was never separated from these essential divine maternal attributes even as she acquired additional traits through the Iron Age and into the Christian era.

The fluidity of oral mythology makes it hard to sort out specific attributes of Celtic deities and relationships among them. Without clearly defined domains, the deities' spheres of influence often overlap. Thus, Brigid shares the Mother Goddess's attribute of protecting of cattle and fertility with other primary goddesses such as Boann and The Morrigan. The fluidity of the mythology also makes it impossible to pin down familial relationships among the deities. The myths generally identify the principal god, The Dagda, as Brigid's father, but they remain undecided about her mother, whom they identify as either Boann or The Morrigan. But it may be that The Dagda is not Brigid's father after all. Some myths say that Brigid is The Dagda's consort, while others identify her as his mother, either of which would make sense if Brigid were herself the Mother Goddess. As to Brigid's offspring, she is sometimes said to have a single son, Ruadan, from her marriage to King Bres, while other myths identify the couple as the parents of Brian, Iuchar, and Iucharba. Another tradition says that the three are Brigid's sons by another father, Tuirenn, while still other sources identify the three sons of Brigid and Tuirenn as Goibniu, Credne, and Luchta, the "Three Gods of Craft." If that's not confusing enough, the Three Gods of Craft are also said to be the sons of Danu. In short, there is no definitive Who's Who in Irish mythology.

## The Goddess of Sovereignty

Despite the ambiguity of attributes and relationships among the Tuatha de Danaan, certain of Brigid's aspects remained consistent as she evolved from Mother Goddess to culture goddess during the Iron Age to the Christian St. Brigid. Perhaps one reason for Brigid's longevity is that she is always associated with benign and nurturing qualities. The traits she embodies align with those Jung identifies with the "good mother": "maternal solicitude and sympathy; the magic authority of the female principle; the wisdom and spiritual exaltation that transcends reason; also, all that is benign, all that cherishes and sustains, furthers growth and fertility."[1]

Similarly, in a mythology that identifies the features of the natural world with goddesses, Brigid is always associated with the beneficent aspects of nature, like the warmth of early spring that renews fertility. The fierce, destructive aspects of nature and fate were represented by other goddesses, like The Morrigan, the triple goddess whose maternal associations with cattle and fertility were offset by her connection with fate and battle. The extremes of nature were often depicted as a dyad of goddesses, with Brigid representing the benign polarity and the fierce nature goddess called The Cailleach as her opposite. Scottish myth portrayed the tension between winter and spring as a rivalry between Brigid, who brought spring and renewed fertility, and the Cailleach, who brought winter and hardship. The power of the ferocious Cailleach was also portrayed through her ability to rearrange the landscape. In Ireland, hilltop cairns are said to have been dropped out of her apron as she flew across the landscape, while hills and mountains in Scotland are said to have been created from rocks the Cailleach dropped from her basket as she strode across the land.

The Cailleach's fiendish reputation was matched by her fearsome appearance:

> Her face was blue-black, of the lustre of coal,
> And her bone tufted tooth was like rusted bone.
> In her head was one deep pool-like eye
> Swifter than a star in winter.
> Upon her head gnarled brushwood
> like the clawed old wood of the aspen root.

## The Sovereignty Union

The identification of the forces of nature with the Feminine was embodied in the "sovereignty union," a king's symbolic marriage to a goddess representing the land. The sovereignty union was so central to kingship that the Irish language did not have a word for the coronation of a king. It was called "the wedding feast of the king."[2] Any man who aspired to kingship had to have his worth validated by such a marriage. A king's fitness to rule depended entirely on the health of his "marriage" to the goddess. Land that failed to prosper was a sign that the king had not taken proper care of his "wife" and was no longer worthy to remain its sovereign. In *Lebor Gabala Erenn (The Book of the Taking of Ireland*, abbreviated *LGE*), Brigid's marriage to Bres the Beautiful validates his sovereignty as king of the Tuatha de Danaan, but his subsequent abuse of his subjects invalidates his sovereignty and causes his shameful deposition from office.

An eleventh century tale, "The Adventures of the Sons of Eochaid Mugmedón," illustrates the nature of the obstacle a man had to overcome to achieve a sovereignty union. The tale concerns the sovereignty union of Niall of the Nine Hostages, who was destined to become Ireland's most legendary king. Eochaid, the High King of Tara, had five sons, four by his queen, and Niall, his love child by his mistress. The story begins with the queen's demand that Eochaid name his successor, clearly hoping that he will name one of her sons as heir to his realm. But instead of caving in to the queen's demand, Eochaid sends all five of his sons into the wilderness on an adventure.

> The five sons of Eochaid went out hunting. They ranged far away from home, and hunted through a part of the country that none of them had seen before. They caught some game and made a fire to cook what they had killed, but they had brought no water with them. After they had eaten, they were struck with a powerful thirst.
>
> They sent the youngest, Fergus, to go out for water, and he looked high and low and could find

nothing. At last he found a well, but barring his way was a woman. She was no ordinary woman; she was a hag. She had long, skinny limbs that were crooked and her skin was spotted with disease and black with dirt. She had fingernails so long they curled and dirt underneath them, mossy teeth that stuck out at all angles like gravestones and hair that was greasy and coarse as a horse's mane. Fergus plucked up the courage to ask this fearsome creature if he could have a drink of water from the well. She said "Yes, you may. If you give me a kiss." Fergus declared that he would rather die of thirst and away he ran. He told his brothers that he had found nothing.

Each of the brothers in turn went looking for water, and each in turn found the well, and the hag. Aillil and Brian refused her. Fiachra managed to bring himself to give her a peck on the cheek, and she was quite pleased with this. She told him that two of his descendants would one day be kings, but she wouldn't give him any water. Each one of the brothers reported to the others that they had found no water at all.

At last Niall went looking, and when he found the hag and she told him her price, he said "Not only will I kiss you, I will lie down with you," and he took her in his arms. When he embraced her, she was transformed into the most beautiful woman, with long straight limbs and white soft skin and golden hair and beautiful rosy lips. He asked, 'What art thou?' She replied, 'King of Tara, I am Sovereignty. . . And your seed shall be over every clan.' She sent him back to his brothers with water from the well, but cautioned him not to let them have any until they swore to give him dominion over them forever.

He took his time at the well before he came back to his brothers. By now they were dying of thirst, but Niall refused to give them a drop of water until they had given up their rights to kingship and renounced their claim to be king. Then they all journeyed back to Tara together.

Niall became the King and to ensure peace in his reign, he conquered all the provinces of Ireland and provinces in Britain and Scotland. Rather than rule over these lands, he took a hostage from each province, nine in total, to ensure that they would not cause any trouble. And all the kings of Ireland after that were descended from Niall of the Nine Hostages.[3]

The sovereignty union was based on an understanding that a successful human society required a vital relationship with the natural world. The man who aspired to kingship had to master his fear and loathing of the most terrifying aspects of the feminine powers of nature in order to be served by those powers. The sovereignty union represented the viable, dynamic relationship between masculine and feminine powers that fostered the well-being of the tribe.

The archetypal sovereignty union was that of The Dagda and The Morrigan. The Dagda's endless versatility as tribal chief was attested by his epithets of "The Good God," "All-Father," and "Lord of Great Knowledge." The scope of his protection was also expressed in the three magical accessories he possessed: a massive club with one end that killed and another that restored life; a cauldron that was never empty; and a harp that could control human emotions or change the seasons. The Morrigan commanded a similarly impressive array of talents, ranging from maternal associations with milk, cattle, sexuality, and fertility to identification with the brutal realities of prophecy, war, fate, and death.

Their coupling is described in *Caith Mag Tuired* (*"The Battle of Moytura,"* abbreviated *CMT)*. The text says that the two had prearranged a meeting at the river near The Dagda's house about the time of Samhain. The Dagda arrived to find The Morrigan straddling the river with her legs wide apart, washing her genitals. The power of her stance was amplified by her hairstyle of "nine loosened tresses on her head," or thrice the sacred number three. After their coupling, they channeled the energy of their sexual union into the safeguarding of the tribe by collaborating on plans for protection of the Tuatha de Danaan in war. The Morrigan's prophetic gift enabled her to pinpoint the spot where the enemy would ford the river. She swore that she would deprive the enemy king of "the blood of his heart and the kidneys of his valor" and promised that when she had done, this she would give "two handfuls of that blood to [the Danaans] that were waiting at the ford of the [river]." The union of these two formidable beings was ritually reenacted annually at Samhain as part of the celebration of the Celtic New Year, to ensure the continuing prosperity of the tribe in the coming year.

## Brigid in the Myths

In transcribing the oral myths, the monastic scribes added their own devices to connect native tradition with Christian history. Their most important collection of poetry and prose was *Lebor Gabala Erenn,* which purported to be the history of Ireland. Oral tradition maintained that Ireland had been colonized by five successive waves of "invaders" from across the sea—the Partholonians, the Nemedeans, the Fir Bolg, the Tuatha de Danaan, and the Milesians. To anchor that tradition to a Christian framework, the scribes added a sixth set of colonists, a fictional, mostly female group led by a granddaughter of Noah called Cessair. *LGE* attests that the first four colonizing groups were wiped out or forced to abandon the island. Possession of the island came down to a contest between the semidivine Tuatha de Danaan and the Milesians, who represent the Irish people (the Gaels).

Brigid is one of the Tuatha de Danaan, who arrive from the north in three hundred ships, which they burn when they reach the island. Unlike previous colonists who were agriculturalists and warriors, the Danaans rely on their "talent," or the powers of Druidry and magic learned during their sojourn in the northern islands of the world. This "talent" includes "magic and every sort of craft and liberal art, so that they were learned, wise, and well skilled in every branch of these arts" (*LGE,* IV). Brigid is patron of these arts and of the segment of society that includes Druidic knowledge, artisanal skills, and other specialized professional knowledge—the *áes dána,* or "people of art."

Brigid first appears in the narrative in connection with sovereignty. The Danaans' king, Nuada, suffers the loss of an arm in battle. The god of healing replaces Nuada's missing limb with an arm (or hand) of silver, and the Danaans want him to continue as their king. But someone remembers Brigid's decree that no physically imperfect man can rule the Danaans; therefore, the disfigured Nuada is no longer eligible to be king. To replace him, the Danaans choose Bres the Beautiful, the incomparably brave and handsome son of a Danaan mother and a Fomorian father. Bres's sovereignty is validated through his marriage to Brigid.

Brigid's influence pervades the next phase of the Danaans' quest for mastery of Ireland. The Tuatha de Danaans have to fight the supernatural Fomorians, who early myths depicted as monstrous beings representing the destructive powers of nature: chaos, darkness, death, blight and drought. By the time of this war, however, the Fomorians have assumed the form of beautiful humans, similar to the Danaans. In the conflict, the Danaans rely on their magical and Druidic "talent" to unleash an array of magical resources against the Fomorians. When the Fomorians notice that the Danaans seem to have an inexhaustible supply of weapons and that Danaan warriors slain in battle reappear on the battlefield the next day as good as new, they dispatch Ruadan, the Fomorian-sympathizing son of Brigid and Bres, as a spy. Ruadan returns from his mission to report the magical wonders he has seen. Slain Danaan warriors are being restored to life by immersion in a magic well over which physicians chant healing incantations. Meanwhile, in the heat of the Danaan smithy, the three Gods of Craft—Goibniu, Luchta, and Credne—are producing weapons at an uncanny pace. After hearing Ruadan's report, the Fomorians send him back to the smithy to shut down the making of weapons by killing the smith Goibniu. But the plan goes tragically wrong. Goibniu turns Ruadan's own spear against him and kills him instead.

Until this point in the narrative, Brigid has remained mostly unseen, but her influence has been strongly felt through her connection with sovereignty, supernatural healing, and magical craftsmanship. With Ruadan's death, however, Brigid arrives at center stage: "Brig(id) came and keened for her son. At first she shrieked, in the end she wept. Then for the first time weeping and shrieking were heard in Ireland" (*CMT* 125). Her wailing is said to inaugurate the ritual of keening for the dead (from *caoineadh,* meaning "to cry, to weep") that will be adopted by grieving women ever afterward. She is also credited with inventing a special whistle for signaling at night. Her connection with the sacred realm of sound is further emphasized in reports that her royal beasts—a pair of oxen, the king of boars, and the king of wethers—cry out to give alarm whenever trouble looms in the land (LGE, IV).

Brigid's connections with governance, skilled craftsmanship, and poetic inspiration in these myths reflect the priorities of a diversifying Iron Age culture. Julius Caesar's account of Gaulish religion in the first century B.C.E. indicates that Brigid was a pan-Celtic goddess in continental Europe. For the benefit of his Roman audience, Caesar identifies six principal Celtic deities with gods of the Roman pantheon. Although none of the deities are identified by their Celtic names, the pantheon he presents contains only a single goddess, and he equates her with Minerva, the Roman goddess of wisdom, medicine, and poetry who "teaches the elements of industry and the arts" (*De Bellico Gallico,* Book 6). Brigid is the only Celtic goddess who matches this description.

A passage written in Ireland nearly a thousand years after the time of Julius Caesar also identifies Brigid with wisdom, medicine, poetry, and "the elements of industry and the arts." *Cormac's Glossary* describes her as:

> ... a poetess, daughter of the Dagda. This is Brigit
> the female sage, or woman of wisdom, i.e., Brigit

the goddess whom poets adored, because very great and very famous was her protecting care. It is therefore they call her goddess of poets by this name. Whose sisters were Brigit the female physician [woman of leechcraft], Brigit the female smith [woman of smithwork]; from whose names with all the Irish a goddess was called Brigit. Brigit, then, breo-aigit, breo-shaigit 'a fiery arrow.'

The attributes of the three sister Brigids suggest that by the Iron Age, the all-encompassing protection once identified with the Mother Goddess had diversified into specializations. The Mother Goddess's universal protection of all people became Brigid the Sage's patronage of poets and the learned "people of art"; the Mother's healing powers were refined into the specialized skills of Brigid the Physician; the Mother's guardianship of the fire of the domestic hearth expanded to encompass supervision of the alchemy of the metalsmith's forge by Brigid the Smith.

### The Sacred Elements: Fire and Water

The entry in *Cormac's Glossary* also extends the controlled fire of the domestic hearth to metaphors of fire harnessed for the benefit of culture. It links each Brigid with a particular aspect of the transformational power of fire: the "fire in the head" of poetic inspiration, the bodily flame of healing, and the annealing fires of the forge. Brigid's associations with the element of fire, like her ties with nature, are always seen as beneficent rather than destructive. The *Glossary's* claim that Brigid's name derives from a root meaning *"a fiery arrow"* is not an actual etymology, but it contains a germ of truth. The sudden spark of inspiration that can kindle a fire in the mind of a poet is as swift and direct as the flight of a flaming arrow. The fiery arrow is also an apt metaphor for Brigid's delivery of the sun's fertility-renewing warmth to Earth in early spring. Egyptian murals from fourteenth century B.C.E. Amarna, the period when Pharaoh Akhenaten attempted to establish monotheistic worship of the sun god Aten, depict solar fire in the form of arrows. The sun god's beneficence to humanity is transferred in a shower of arrowlike rays extending from the solar disk toward Earth, with each arrow ending in a tiny, open hand.

Brigid has traditionally been assigned guardianship of the household fire, the focal point for the feminine gifts of nourishment, warmth, sacred hospitality, and human connection. As metalworking and craftsmanship were developed to high levels during the Iron Age, Brigid's protection of the hearth fire at the center of the home expanded to make her the guardian spirit of the smithy. She was mistress of both the fire of the forge and the special knowledge smiths required in their craft. The arcane knowledge smiths mastered to enable them to transform raw metals dug out of the earth into objects of utility and beauty by passing them through fire made them initiates into Brigid's domain. The skills they exhibited in the pursuit of their craft were so astonishing that the common folk came to regard them as wizards. A poem ascribed to St. Patrick reflects the superstitious awe that surrounded them in calling upon God for protection from the "spells of women, smiths and druids."[4]

Brigid's associations with solar fire also linked her with the faculty of vision. The Celts saw the sun as a great eye whose gaze could bring fertility to the Earth or destroy crops and vegetation. Brigid represented the life-giving, beneficent aspects of that great eye. Its destructive potential was represented by the terrible Balor, the leader of the demonic Fomorians who "had a single eye in his forehead, a venomous fiery eye. There were always seven coverings over this eye. One by one Balor removed the coverings. With the first covering the bracken began to wither, with the second the grass became copper-coloured, with the third the woods and timber began to heat, with the fourth smoke came from the trees, with the fifth everything grew red, with the sixth it sparked. With the seventh, they were all set on fire, and the whole countryside was ablaze!"[5]

Brigid's associations with the benign aspects of vision became especially closely tied to human eyesight in the legends of St. Brigid, who was known for her ability to heal eye diseases and restore sight to the blind. The faculty of eyesight appears in the legend that Brigid disqualified herself from marriage by plucking out one of her eyes. (The hagiographers who report this grisly deed are quick to reassure readers that the saint's great piety caused her eye to be restored to her afterward.) The sacrifice of physical vision as the price of gaining inner vision is a prominent motif in many myths, such as the story of Odin, the great All-Father of Norse mythology. Odin's relentless quest for knowledge took him to the well of wisdom sheltered in the roots of the great world tree, Yggdrasil. The well was guarded by Mimir, the wisest of all beings, who had attained cosmic knowledge by drinking the waters of the well. When Odin asked Mimir if he might be granted a drink from the well, he was told that it would cost him one eye. Without hesitation, Odin gouged out one of his eyes and dropped it into the well, whereupon Mimir permitted him a drink of the water of wisdom.

## The Well of Wisdom

The naming of many rivers for goddesses attests the connection between the feminine and flowing waters. The River Boyne, for example, takes its name from Boann, the goddess who is sometimes identified as Brigid's mother. Ireland's most important river, the Shannon, is named for the goddess Sinann, who is sometimes conflated with Brigid. Sinann's story is a tragic one. She was endowed with all gifts except the gift of wisdom, but because of this, she desired wisdom above all else. She had been warned not to approach the Well of Wisdom, but her desire made her reckless. When she drew near the well, it broke from its bounds in a great flood, drowning Sinann and carrying her out to the sea. Mythologically, the story of Sinann's fate can be read as a creation myth in which the river goddess sacrifices herself to establish the land's fertility.[6] Folklore, on the other hand, has taken another track, treating Sinann's tragic end as a cautionary tale warning women of the dangers of seeking wisdom.

The Irish myths' depiction of wisdom as an essence residing in the flowing waters of certain rivers, springs, or "wells of wisdom" is closely related to Indo-European mythology in which certain bodies of water contain a rare, potent, brightly burning essence that was avidly sought by poets for its ability to convey extraordinary powers of wisdom and poetic inspiration.[7] The Irish word translated as "wisdom" is *imbas,* which has the dual meaning of "all knowledge" and "great inspiration." Mythological wells of wisdom could be identified by the sacred hazel trees that surrounded them. The ripened nuts of the sacred hazel trees fell into the water, where they were eaten by the salmon of wisdom who lived there. The *Dindshenchas* ("Lore of Places") describes a well of wisdom:

The nine hazels of Crimall the sage
drop their fruits yonder under the well. . . .
Together grow, in unwonted fashion,
their leaves and their flowers:
— a wonder is this, though a noble quality,
and a wonder their ripening all in a moment.
When the cluster of nuts is ripe
they fall down into the well:
they scatter below on the bottom,
and the salmon eat them.
From the juice of the nuts (no paltry matter)
are formed the mystic bubbles;
thence come momently the bubbles
down the green-flowing streams.

*Imbas* could be ingested either by drinking the water
of a sacred well or by eating one of the salmon of wisdom
that swam there. But *imbas* was not available to all comers.
It was considered a gift granted only by divine consent, and
some seekers pursued it for many years without success.
One such seeker of wisdom was a poet named Finnegas. It
had been prophesied that Finnegas was destined to eat the
salmon that lived in a certain pool of the Boyne and ate the
sacred hazelnuts and that afterward "nothing would remain
unknown to him." Finnegas had spent seven long years
trying to catch the salmon, and finally one day he attained
his prize. He handed the salmon to the young boy who was
living with him, one Fionn mac Cumhaill (Finn McCool),
and told him to cook it for him. While Fionn was cooking
the salmon, he burned his thumb and reflexively put the
thumb in his mouth to soothe the pain. The salmon's
wisdom flowed immediately into Fionn, and for the rest of

his life, Fionn could access all knowledge by simply reciting a charm and placing his thumb in his mouth.

As "woman of wisdom," Brigid had a unique relationship with sacred water sources and the wisdom they contained. Her associations with the sacred elements of fire, water, and wisdom converge in a tale called "Cormac's Adventures in the Land of Promise." Brigid neither appears in the tale, nor is she mentioned by name, but her influence pervades it throughout. The story concerns Cormac mac Art, the wisest of all the High Kings of Ireland. The king is granted a visit to "The Land of Promise," the magical Otherworld of the Tuatha Dé Danaan. His adventures begin when he encounters a mysterious stranger carrying a marvelous silver branch with three golden apples that make an entrancing music. The tinkling, hypnotic music of the golden apples causes the king to fall into a deep sleep. When he awakens, he finds himself in a misty, dreamlike place. The mysterious figure with the magic musical apples reveals himself to be none other than Manannán mac Lir, King of the Land of Promise. He confides to Cormac, king to king, that he has brought him to the Land of Promise to show him the wonders of this marvelous "land free of suffering, where no one ages, and no one dies, and no one ever falls ill."

Among the marvels Cormac sees in the Land of Promise is a well out of which flow five shining streams, whose waters make a lilting music more exquisite than any music ever heard on Earth. The marvelous well is surrounded by nine purple hazel trees, the symbols of divine knowledge. As the nuts of the sacred hazel trees ripen, they fall into the well, where they are eaten by the five salmon of wisdom. Manannán mac Lir explains that the five streams flowing out from the well are the five physical senses through which everyone may obtain knowledge. But he reveals that true wisdom is granted only to those who drink from the sacred well. "Everyone drinks from the streams," he explains, "but only poets, skilled ones, and the people of art drink from both the streams and the spring itself."[8] The people he is describing, of course, are the *áes dána,* the learned ones who are under Brigid's special protection.

The statement suggests that by the medieval period, the benign aspects of the Divine Feminine were consistently projected onto her. As Brigid was reimagined in the Christian era as St. Brigid of Kildare, the protective and nurturing qualities of the Irish goddess coalesced into a figure who was the beloved mother of the Irish Church, protectress of her people, and Co-Mother of God.

# Chapter Three
# "The Saint of Their Desire"

Brigit, excellent woman,
a flame golden, delightful,
May (she), the sun dazzling splendid,
bear us to the eternal kingdom!
May Brigit save us beyond throngs of demons!
May she overthrow before us
(the) battles of every disease!
May she destroy within us our flesh's taxes
The branch with blossoms, the mother of Jesus!
                St. Ultan's *Hymn to Brigid*, 7th century

The tradition that Ireland was "taken" or conquered by six successive waves of incomers from across the sea is at least partly true. Archaeology and DNA research confirm that Ireland was indeed settled by people from other parts of the world. But no weapons have been discovered that would support the notion that any of these waves of immigration were actually hostile invasions. It appears that over the centuries, a series of immigrant groups adopted Celtic language and culture and were simply absorbed into the population. When Ireland was finally "taken" by Christianity, the conquest was entirely bloodless, but it took more than four centuries.

A story in the ninth-century *Book of Armagh* relates that the two daughters of King Loiguire arose one morning and went to the Well of Clebach to perform their customary ablutions. When they reached the well, they were surprised to find a group of unknown men gathered there. The strangers were none other than St. Patrick and a "holy assembly of bishops."

The young women "did not know whence they were or of what shape or from what people or from what region, but thought they were *sidhe* (fairy) men or earth-gods or a phantom; and the maidens said to them: 'Whence are you and whence have you come?' and Patrick said to them: 'It would be better for you to profess our true God than to ask questions about our race.' The first maiden said: 'Who is God and where is God and whose God is he and where is his dwelling-place? Has your God sons and daughters, gold and silver? Is he ever-living, is he beautiful, has he many fostered his son, are his daughters dear and beautiful in the eyes of the men of the earth? Is he in the sky or in the earth or in the water, in rivers, in mountains, in valleys?'"

This story suggests how exceedingly strange the early Christians must have seemed to the native Gaels. The newcomers tried to persuade the people to trade their age-old confidence in the sacredness of the natural world for the teachings of a holy book that the Irish, not being literate, could not even read for themselves. Converting the hearts and minds of people who saw sacredness in every rock and spring in the landscape to the Christian view that nature was the creation of a transcendent God who lived somewhere beyond this world was an enormous shift. It is hardly surprising that Ireland's conversion took such a long time.

Christian writings from the seventh-century hint at the kinds of resistance the missionaries met. The seventh-century *Penitentials of Theodoris* insisted that "no one shall go to trees, or wells, or stones or enclosures, or anywhere else except to God's church, and there make vows or release himself from them." In a similar vein, St. Eligius decreed that "no Christian place lights at the temples or at the stones, or at fountains and springs, or at trees, or at places where three ways meet . . . Let no one presume to purify by sacrifice, or to enchant herbs, or to make flocks pass through a hollow tree or an aperture in the earth; for by so doing he seems to consecrate them to the devil."

In 601 C.E., Pope Gregory wrote letters of pastoral advice to the missionaries who were attempting to convert Celtic tribes in England. The Holy Father counseled Augustine of Canterbury to substitute Christian rituals for the traditional cattle sacrifices of the Celtic Britons. He advised Augustine's associate, Abbot Mellitus, to adopt the practical strategy of repurposing sacred pagan sites:

> I have come to the conclusion that the temples of the idols in England should not on any account be destroyed. Augustine must smash the idols, but the temples themselves should be sprinkled with holy water and the altars set up in them in which relics are to be enclosed. For we ought to take advantage of well-built temples by purifying them from devil-worship and dedicating them to the service of the true God. In this way, I hope the

people, seeing their temples are not destroyed, will leave their idolatry and yet continue to frequent the places as formerly, so coming to know and revere the true God.

Accordingly, churchmen did their best to redefine traditional practices as Christian rituals, reconsecrate temples as churches, and rededicate holy wells associated with Celtic deities to Christian saints. They transformed native deities into saints and made the less benign ones into demons. The Tuatha de Danaan were reduced into the *sidhe,* or fairy folk, the mischievous sprites called "the Good People." "Pagan," a word that originally meant simply "the religion of country people," took on pejorative overtones of heresy, heathenism and hedonism. Practices the Church found it impossible to assimilate, like the Druid tradition of a married priesthood and the custom of baptizing children in milk, were labeled "pagan" and gradually phased out.

St. Brigid of Kildare might be a poster girl for this Christian syncretism. The church idealized her as a servant of Christ and mother of Irish Christianity, yet the legends her biographers used as evidence of her piety incorporated the very attributes the Irish venerated in their goddess. St. Brigid was easily seen as the provident Great Mother who guarded the welfare of cattle and used the staple foods of milk and butter to perform miraculous feedings of the hungry. If no dairy products were on hand, she was capable of conjuring nourishing food from inedible substances like pine bark. She sought justice for the poor, healed all kinds of disease, and oversaw the fertility of women. Her protection of the churches and monasteries under her authority, her *paruchia,* reflected the Sovereignty of the goddess. Many of the miraculous stories of her life included the sacred elements of fire and water.

Many legends about St. Brigid have been preserved in the hagiographies created by medieval Christian writers. I refer to these half-dozen works collectively as the *Lives*. The first of these, *Vitae Sanctae Brigidae ("The Life of Saint Brigid," VSB)* was written about 650 C.E. by Cogitosus, a monk of Kildare Abbey. Cogitosus and the writers who followed never questioned the miracle-filled legends about Brigid that had been handed down to them. Modeling their texts on the New Testament gospels, they presented Brigid's miraculous healings and multiplications of food as parallels to the miracles of Jesus. Among the *Lives'* claims about Brigid were stories that she could change the weather or move a massive millstone across many miles from quarry to abbey and reports of several occasions throughout her life when fire unexpectedly burst from her head. For the writers of the *Lives,* such improbable manifestations required no corroborating evidence; they were simply proof of Brigid's incomparable holiness.

Nearly a thousand years after St. Brigid's lifetime, by which time the Irish church had become thoroughly Romanized, the saint was venerated as the apotheosis of submissive Christian womanhood. Here is a tribute to her from *An Leabhar Breac ("The Speckled Book")*:

> There was not in the world one of more bashfulness and modesty than this holy virgin. She never washed her hands, or her feet, or head before men. She never looked a man in the face. She never spoke without blushing. She was abstinent, unblemished, fond of prayer, patient, rejoicing in God's commands, benevolent, humble,

forgiving, charitable. She was a consecrated shrine for the preservation of the Body of Christ. She was a temple of God. Her heart and mind were the throne of the Holy Spirit; she was meek before God. She was distressed with the miserable. She was bright in miracles. And hence in things created her type is the Dove among birds, the Vine amongst trees, and the Sun above the stars.

The pious, submissive woman lauded in this encomium bears little resemblance to the Brigid depicted in the *Lives*. While the *Lives* are unceasing in their praise for Brigid's virtues of piety, compassion for the poor, and miracle-working, the figure they portray was far too energetic to pose with bowed head upon a pedestal. She would hardly have had time to guard her modesty before men when she was traveling around the land, perhaps even across the Irish Sea, to found new churches and monastic communities. Neither was she submissive to any earthly master. When justice was at stake, she did not hesitate to defy men in authority. While she was steadfastly obedient to God, the Brigid depicted in the *Lives* is a rebel, pioneer, and all-around "uppity woman," with more than a little of the goddess clinging to her.

The *Lives* also overflow with the liminal energy of the Divine Feminine. They bring to life a hinge point in history when pagan polytheism and Christianity danced their dance of conflict and compromise. Almost every episode of Brigid's life reflects a tension between traditional ways and the new era introduced by Christianity. The tension begins with her conception by a pagan chieftain and an enslaved Christian woman in his household. Brigid is born on a threshold at sunrise. Her life involves her in dealings with the authority figures of both Christian and pagan worlds—Druids, kings, and bishops. In her roles as midwife and deathbed consoler, she presides over the thresholds of birth and death.

Brigid's mother, Broisech, is a slave owned by her father, Dubthach, a prosperous pagan client chieftain of the King of Leinster. When Dubthach's jealous wife demands that he get rid of his pregnant concubine, he reluctantly agrees to sell Broisech, with the stipulation that the unborn child she carries will be a free person. After she is sold to a Druid, Broisech is working on his farm when she gives birth at the moment she is crossing a threshold just as the sun is rising. She baptizes her daughter with the pail of fresh milk she has just collected. From the moment of birth, Brigid is linked to both Druidism and dairy culture. When she is weaned and proves unable to tolerate human food, the Druid solves the problem by procuring a white cow with red ears, whose markings identify her as a magic cow from Otherworld. Young Brigid thrives on the milk of the Otherworld cow, milked by her Christian foster mother.

The *Lives* agree that St. Brigid was born on February 1, the goddess Brigid's traditional festival of Imbolc, in the province of Leinster in the year 452 C.E. She is also said to have died on February 1, although the sources place the year of her death variously at 524, 526, or 528. Beyond these slender anchor points, however, stories of her life depart from historical chronology and partake of the mythic legends of semidivine beings. Her birth is surrounded with the kinds of signs and wonders that announce the birth of a Divine Child. She radiates solar fire while she is still in the womb. Her future preeminence is prophesied even before her birth by Druids of the old faith and bishops of the new. From childhood she reveals a talent for miraculous multiplications of food. The double monastery she establishes and administers as an abbess develops a reputation as a center of learning, healing, and art throughout the land. Her numerous manifestations of the Goddess's protection of fertility culminate in her role as the midwife and mother of Irish Christianity.

St. Brigid's baptism in milk and weaning to the milk of an Otherworld cow establish her links with the cattle-based culture of medieval Ireland. At a time when owning a single cow could mean the difference between survival and starvation, Brigid's legendary generosity focused on cattle. She gave cows to the needy, provided grazing land for cattle, induced cows to produce extraordinary quantities of milk and butter, and even foiled the crimes of cattle thieves. She was said to be able to produce several basketfuls of butter from a single churning, enable a cow to be milked three times in a single day, and, in one case when no cow was handy, to provide an ailing nun with curative fresh milk produced from a glass of water. Beyond her marvelous ways with milk and butter, she transformed water into beer and conjured food from inedible substances. One legend adds a unique twist to Jesus's feeding of multitudes by reporting that Brigid fed a crowd with twelve loaves of bread—and a *sheep!*

From the time she was a child, Brigid's habit of giving away anything she could get her hands on earned her a reputation as a delinquent. When her elders challenged her appropriation of anything that wasn't nailed down, she would reply that she was just following the command of Christ. She reasoned that he would want his children to have what they needed, and besides, everything belonged to him in the first place. Once, after Brigid's exasperated stepmother complained that she was stealing everything in the house to give to the poor, her father put Brigid into his chariot and took her to the King of Leinster with the intention of selling her to him as a slave. When they reached the king's house, Dubthach took off the jewel-hilted sword that had been a gift from the king, in order not to offend the king by coming before him armed, and left the sword in the chariot with Brigid. While Dubthach was with the king, a beggar came along and asked Brigid for alms. Since she had nothing else to give him, she gave him the only thing in the chariot—her father's sword. When Dubthach returned and found the sword gone, he was incensed. The sword was a priceless item, a gift of the king himself. What had the girl been thinking? Brigid calmly explained that she had given the sword to Christ. Her reasoning persuaded the king that Brigid was not destined for a life of slavery, and after giving Dubthach another sword to replace the one his generous daughter had given to Christ, he sent them both back home. This reckless generosity continued throughout Brigid's life. As abbess, she was famous for giving away any resource at hand—food, a horse, a cow, jewelry, and once, even a bishop's vestments. Cogitosus, who clearly admired Brigid's generosity, wrote that her one desire was "to satisfy the poor, to expel every hardship, to spare every miserable man."

## Healing and Sovereignty

In addition to her legendary generosity, St. Brigid was widely celebrated for her abilities as a healer, curing leprosy, blindness, paralysis, deafness, muteness, bulimia, and demonic possession. She helped infertile women to conceive and ensured the safe deliveries of their infants. She was even reported to restore a man's missing hand, like the mythological Miach, who replaced the silver hand of King Nuada with one of flesh and blood. Water featured prominently in Brigid's healings. She healed a bent-over man by sending him to bathe in the river, cured lepers by washing them, and healed a crippled man by bathing his feet in morning dew. Her girdle dipped in water could convey healing to the sick in distant places, and a single drop of water from Brigid's mantle was said to create an entire lake with healing powers.

Her affinity with the feminine element of water is also demonstrated in her ability to locate underground sources of water for thirsty travelers, allow her nuns to cross flooded rivers without harm, and even change the course of a river. She could also control the weather. She was able to provide clear skies for the Abbey's reapers at harvest time when it was raining heavily everywhere else. *Bethu Brigte* recounts an occasion when Brigid went out to pasture some sheep when a terrible storm was raging. She stilled the rain and wind with a song:

> Grant me a clear day
> for Thou art a dear friend, a kingly youth;
> for the sake of Thy mother, loving Mary,
> ward off rain, ward off wind.

> My king will do [it] for me,
> rain will not fall till the night,
> on account of Brigit today,
> who is going here to the herding.

St. Brigid also deserved the Mother Goddess's epithet "Lady of Beasts." Besides her affinity with domestic animals, her influence induced untamed animals to behave in ways contrary to their wild natures. After she blessed a wild boar, it remained docilely among her herd "unafraid and tame because even the brute beasts and animals could not resist her words and wishes"*(VPSB, §107)*. A herd of pigs donated to the Abbey was delivered by a pack of wild wolves that drove them there "through reverence for blessed Brigid" *(VSB, §19)*. She summoned wild ducks to her hand simply for the pleasure of petting them *(VSB, §21)*. That her affinity for animals lingered for centuries after her death was attested by Gerald of Wales' twelfth-century description of "Brigid's bird," a graceful falcon that habitually perched atop the Kildare church tower (*Topographia Hibernica*, XXXVII). Cogitosus summarizes: "And from all this, it can be clearly understood that the whole of nature, beasts, cattle, and birds, was subjected to her power" *(VSB, §21)*.

The *Lives* portray a formidable woman who was always ready to intervene on behalf of the ordinary people under her protection. She recovered stolen property, foiled the nefarious intentions of thieves, exposed prevarication, and settled disputes. When the cause was just, she would stand up to fathers, brothers, bishops, or kings. As an abbess in an era when the heads of monasteries were the most important figures in the Irish church, Brigid exercised an exceptional degree of power. Cogitosus boasts that Kildare Abbey is "head of almost all the Irish Churches with supremacy over all the monasteries of the Irish and its *paruchia* extends over the whole land of Ireland, reaching from sea to sea"*(VSB, §4)*.

Brigid's Divine Feminine powers of sovereignty were symbolized by her cloak or mantle. The miraculous powers of her cloak were revealed in her confrontation with a king over a piece of land. The Abbey was located on the Curragh Plain, some of the richest farmland in Ireland, and all of it belonged to the King of Leinster. Brigid approached the king to ask for a bit of his vast acreage for grazing land for the Abbey's sheep and cattle, but he refused her request. Brigid took a moment to pray, then she revised her petition. She asked if the Abbey could have only as much land as her mantle would cover. The king agreed. After all, he reasoned, what was the Abbey going to do with a square meter of sod? But when Brigid placed her cloak on the ground, it began to stretch and stretch in four directions until it covered the entire Curragh Plain. The astonished king conceded. Brigid could have her land. The image of Brigid's cloak as a great protective blanket spreading across the whole land of Ireland is preserved in many an Irish blessing, such as this:

O Brigid spread above my head
Your mantle bright to guard me.

Brigid's mantle also became integrated into domestic celebrations of Imbolc as an important symbol of her protection, as we will see in Chapter 5.

## Sacred Fire

The sacred flames that surrounded the infant Brigid reappear repeatedly in the *Lives*. *Vita Prima Sanctae Brigitae* relates that a king to whom Brigid had promised victory was about to go into battle when he saw "Saint Brigid going before him into battle with her staff in her right hand and a column of fire was blazing skywards from her head"*(VPSB, §88)*. When Brigid knelt before the bishop at her consecration to have the veil placed on her head, a column of fire shot from her head all the way up to the roof ridge of the chapel. The astonished bishop interpreted this as a sign that he should immediately ordain the young woman kneeling before him as a bishop. Depictions of St. Brigid holding a bishop's crozier in medieval art indicate that she functioned in that capacity during her lifetime, when she presided over communities of both men and women at Kildare Abbey. In later centuries when male clergy were scandalized by the notion of a female bishop, the writer of *Bethu Brigte* came to the rescue by explaining that her consecration had been a mistake; the bishop had been so God-intoxicated that he had simply read from the wrong page in the prayer book!

Brigid is connected with solar fire in another story that also features her cloak. At the end of a day of physical labor, the abbess came back to her quarters, fatigued from working in the fields, and unthinkingly tossed her wet cloak onto what she thought was a tree limb. The assumption was not unreasonable, since branches were often left attached to trees used in the wattle and daub construction of those days to serve as built-in clothes racks. But what had caught the weary abbess's cloak was not a limb; it was a shaft of late afternoon sunlight shining into the house. One version of the story says that the sunbeam continued to shine into the house even after the sun had gone down, so that no one in the house could go to sleep until Brigid had removed her cloak from its hanger.

St. Brigid is also connected with solar fire through the woven cross that bears her name. The equal-armed cross, which has been a solar symbol from primeval times, was attached to the saint through the legend that she invented it on the spot during a pastoral visit to the deathbed of a pagan chieftain. The story says that while Brigid sat talking with the dying man at his bedside, she picked up a handful of rushes from the floor and began to weave them into the shape of a cross. As she busied her hands with her weaving, she told the dying man the story of the Crucifixion, using the cross as a visual aid. The chieftain was reportedly so deeply affected that he was baptized on his deathbed.

St. Brigid's best-known association with fire is undoubtedly with the sacred eternal flame at Kildare Abbey. The sacred fire was never allowed to go out, being tended in turn by nineteen nuns plus Brigid herself. In the twelfth century, some 700 years after the foundation of the Abbey, Gerald of Wales (Giraldus Cambrensis) wrote an eyewitness account of the tending of the sacred fire.

> As in the time of St. Brigit twenty nuns were here engaged in the Lord's warfare, she herself being the twentieth, after her glorious departure, nineteen have always formed the society, the number having never been increased. Each of them has the care of the fire for a single night in turn, and, on the evening before the twentieth night, the last nun, having heaped wood upon the fire, says, 'Brigit, take charge of your own fire; for this night belongs to you.' She then leaves the fire, and in the morning it is found that the fire has not gone out, and that the usual quantity of fuel has been used (*Topographia Hibernica, XXXIV*).

Brigid's sacred flame at Kildare Abbey was briefly extinguished by a thirteenth-century bishop, but thereafter was rekindled and continued to burn without interruption until Henry VIII dissolved the monasteries in the sixteenth century, burning for a thousand years altogether.

If local Irish legends are to be believed, the sacred fire may have burned at Kildare for even longer than a thousand years. Kildare Abbey was said to occupy the site of a former Druid shrine where an eternal fire was tended by nineteen priestesses. The tradition that the sacred fire was maintained by nineteen female guardians points to its possible Druidic origins. The number nineteen is cosmologically significant because it is the number of years it takes for the moon and sun to return to exactly the same positions relative to each other, what is called the metonic cycle. Evidence that the metonic cycle was widely known in the ancient world includes its use in ancient calendars in Babylon and China and its appearances in Classical literature. In Homer's *Odyssey*, for example, the time from Odysseus's departure from Ithaka to his reunion with Penelope is nineteen years, identical with the length of time that passes before the sun and moon are reunited. The metonic cycle also appears in Diodorus's account of an island in the far north inhabited by the legendary race of Hyperboreans to which the sun god Apollo returns every nineteen years. Carvings on a calendar stone at the Boyne Valley Neolithic site of Knowth indicate that the metonic cycle was also known to the pre-Celtic inhabitants of Ireland, and it was certainly known to the astronomically astute Druids.

The eternal flame's ties with Druidism are also suggested by a cryptic detail in Gerald's account. Gerald reports that the fire was the center of a sacred feminine precinct surrounded by a circular hedge of stakes and brushwood that no male could enter upon penalty of "the divine vengeance." A similar taboo against masculine intrusion into a feminine sanctuary appears in Strabo's first-century B.C.E. account of a community of Druidesses living on an island near the mouth of the River Loire. Strabo reports that no men were permitted to set foot within the island's precincts. The nature of the "divine vengeance" is disclosed in Gerald's description of the fate of two men who dared to transgress sacred space: One man lost the use of the leg he had flung across the hedge and the other was stricken with madness (*Topographia Hibernica*, XLVIII).

### "The Saint of Their Desires"

All in all, the saint revealed in the *Lives* is quite a package. She wields extraordinary powers, yet she modestly passes all credit for her miracles to the Christian God. St. Brigid's pedagogically minded hagiographers are never reluctant to cite her miracles as proof of Jesus's affirmation that "everything is possible to one who believes" (*VSB*, §9). A report that Brigid caused the pregnancy of one of her nuns to disappear was attributed to "a strength of faith most powerful and ineffable." Her miraculous changing of water into ale was said to be done by "blessing it with the power of faith." Yet no matter how firmly the *Lives* insist that the powers she channels are from God, something of the pagan goddess is always present in St. Brigid.

One story about the abbess claims that in an emergency she multiplied a single barrel of ale into a supply sufficient for eighteen of her churches for all of Holy Week. A prayer attributed to St. Brigid combines her fame as a brewer and miraculous multiplier of food with her reputation for sacred hospitality. The prayer depicts a lake of ale as the focus of a joyous, inclusive community:

I should like a great lake of beer to give to God.
I should like the angels of Heaven to be tippling
there for all eternity.
I should like the men of Heaven to live with me,
dance and sing.
I'd make men happy for their own sakes.
I should like Jesus to be there, too.
I'd like the people of Heaven to gather from all the
parishes around.
I'd give a special welcome to the women,
the three Marys of great renown.
I'd sit with the men, the women of God,
There by the great lake of beer
We'd be drinking good health forever,
And every drop would be a prayer.

This vision of holy conviviality points to the distinctive character of Celtic Christianity. While the Church appropriated and reshaped many deeply rooted traditions in its attempt to convert Ireland's people, the Church was also changed by its engagement with the Gaelic spirit. Lines by the Welsh poet Ruth Bidgood evoke the unique expression of Christianity that arose from its encounter with the Divine Feminine:

Yet here in the Celtic lands, the new faith dealt
gently with the old. Sometimes it twined about
the primitive stones, enriching them with the
name of Christ and the mark of his cross.

It danced with the dancers,
and let the candle-rays of its festivals merge
with the torchlight of old processions.

It understood its people's bond with the Earth,
and to her children it gave back the mother, in her
gentlest shape— as Mary the mother of Christ, or
as his foster mother, St. Brigid of Ireland, Sant
Ffraid of Wales.

She it was who, story by story, miracle by miracle,
was fashioned by the Celtic peoples into the saint
of their desire.[1]

In St. Brigid, Christianity found a comforting
terrestrial counterpart to the transcendent heavenly Father,
a familiar earthly Mother who was always at hand to look
after the material and spiritual needs of her people, whether
they needed healing, comfort, justice, a milk cow, or simply
a good draught of beer. The *Lives* of Brigit of Kildare show
her to be a thoroughly Celtic incarnation of the Divine
Feminine. And despite the best efforts of St. Brigid's
hagiographers to defer all the credit for her remarkable
works to God, fire came out of her head, and she could
hang her cloak on a beam of sunlight.

# Chapter Four
# Brigid and Mary,
# Co-Mothers of God

Bride is said to preside over fire, over art, over all
beauty. . . . She is the Mary and the Juno of the
Gael.

Alexander Carmichael, *Carmina Gadelica*

A story in *Bethu Brigte* relates that an "old pious nun"
invited young Brigid to speak to a gathering of the faithful.
The two arrived at the meeting just as Bishop Ibor was telling
the assembly about his dream from the previous night.

> "I thought, said he, that I saw this night the Virgin
> Mary in my sleep, and a certain venerable cleric
> said to me: 'This is Mary who will dwell among
> you.' Just then the nun and Brigit walked into the
> assembly. The bishop exclaimed, 'This is the Mary
> who was seen by me in a dream.'"

The identification of Brigid with Mary suggests that
the Irish immediately recognized their own Brigid and the
Holy Mother Mary as archetypes of the Divine Feminine
and explains Brigid's soubriquet of the "Mary of the Gael."
Many of the Hebridean poems and prayers preserved in
the collection *Carmina Gadelica* portray Mary and Bride

as close, sisterly allies. But Alexander Carmichael, the compiler of *Carmina Gadelica*, hints that Brigid may have enjoyed an edge in popularity. In his comments, he writes, "Bride and her services are near to the hearts and lives of the people. In some [ways], she is much more to them than Mary is."[1]

Mary's elevated status in Christianity illustrates the fluidity of the Divine Feminine, particularly its ability to flow through crevices and around obstacles. Christianity was initially a flexible movement that emphasized emulating the "Way" of Jesus Christ rather than adhering to a formulaic set of beliefs. In the early years of the movement, there were many ways to be Christian. But after the year 380 C.E., when Christianity was adopted as the official religion of the Roman Empire, the faith began to morph from a movement into an institution, one that internalized the organizational structure of the declining Empire. It also became hierarchical and far less friendly to Feminine energies. Maintaining that it alone held the keys to the Kingdom of Heaven, the Western Church sought to standardize belief through credal statements adopted by councils of churchmen. These early creeds, which are still recited in churches throughout the world today, centered on a trinitarian, masculine godhead, and any individual who did not assent to these affirmations would remain outside the realm of salvation, labeled a "heretic."

To certify the human bona fides of Jesus, the creeds did mention one female—his mother, Mary. And that's where the Divine Feminine began to penetrate the crevices in the institutional walls. The attributes of the beloved Great Mother, who had never entirely disappeared from the affections of the people, came to be projected onto Mary. Mary was not part of the Holy Trinity or a goddess, but as mother of the god-man Jesus, she became elevated to the position of Mother of God. In 431 C.E., just fifty years after Christianity became the official imperial religion, a church council meeting declared Mary to be "Mother of God." Appropriately, the church council that made this declaration met in Ephesus, whose name means "City of the Mother Goddess." The city is alleged to have been founded by Amazons, and legend claims that Mary herself lived out her last years in a small house near Ephesus. Where better to declare Mary "Mother of God" than in a city overflowing with connections with the Goddess?

When the Church came to Ireland, it brought the Mother of God into a world already brimming with feminine energy. The Gaels readily embraced Mary because they recognized in her the same the Divine Feminine essence embodied in their own Brigid. Then the Gaelic imagination went to work, merging their stories in highly creative ways.

### The Holy Midwife

The strongest bond between Brigid and Mary appears in the belief that Brigid was the midwife who delivered Jesus in the stable at Bethlehem. This tradition was especially strong in the Hebrides, where the midwife, or "knee-woman," was a kind of priestess of childbirth, responsible not only for the safety of mother and child but also for rituals that protected the newborn at the threshold of life. When a woman was in labor, the midwife would stand on the threshold of the house with her hands on the jambs and beseech Brigid (Bride) to come in:

> Bride! Bride! Come in,
> Thy welcome is truly made,
> Give thou relief to the woman,
> And give the conception to the Trinity. *(CG §70)*

As soon as the child was born, the midwife would place three drops of water on the head of the baby in the name of the Christian Trinity. This "knee-woman's baptism" was believed to protect children until they could be formally baptized by clergy, which in remote regions could be a matter of months. The baptism was followed by a pagan ritual in which the newborn was passed back and forth across the fire three times while words were said to the sun god, then carried three times around the fire sunwise (clockwise). Together these rites invoking both Christian and pagan deities were thought to cover all the bases of protection for the newborn. *(CG §217, n.)*

An account of Bride's role in Bethlehem recorded in *Carmina Gadelica* is colored with such details of Hebridean childbirth customs:

> Bride, it is said, was the daughter of poor, pious parents and the serving maid in the inn at Bethlehem. A great drought occurred in the land and the master of the hostelry went away with his cart to get water from afar, leaving Bride a bowl of water and a bannock of bread to sustain her till his return. The man left orders that Bride was not to give food or drink to anyone, as he had left only enough for herself; and she was not to give shelter to anyone until he returned.
>
> However, as Bride was working in the house two strangers came to the door. The man was old, with brown hair and a grey beard, and the woman was young and beautiful, with an oval face, straight nose, blue eyes, red lips, small ears, and golden brown hair which fell below her waist. The strangers asked Bride for a place to rest, for they

were foot sore and weary, for food to satisfy their hunger and for water to quench their thirst. Bride dared not give them shelter, but she did give them her bannock and water from her bowl. The couple ate and drank outside the door, and having thanked Bride the strangers went their way, with Bride gazing wistfully and sorrowfully after them. Bride saw how weary was the young woman and her heart was heavy that she did not have the power to give them shade from the heat of the sun and cover from the cold of the dew. When Bride went back into the inn as dusk began to fall she saw, to her amazement, that the bannock of bread was whole, and the bowl of water was as full as it had been before! She could not believe it! The food and the water that she had given the strangers and had herself seen them consume were as they had been before.

When she recovered from her wonderment Bride went out to look for the pair who had gone on their way, but she couldn't see them. Just then she saw a brilliant golden light shining from the stable door, and realizing it was not a dreag a bhais, (a "meteor of death"), she went into the stable and there she saw the Virgin Mother about to give birth. Bride assisted the mother in the birth of the child, who was Jesus Christ, the son of God who had come to earth and the strangers were Joseph and Mary. When the child was born Bride put three drops of water from the nearby spring of pure water on his forehead, in the name of God, in name of Jesus and in the name of the Holy Spirit. As the innkeeper was returning home he ascended the hill on which the inn stood and suddenly heard the sound of music. This seemed to flow past his inn like a flowing stream, while above his stable he saw a bright star. From these signs he knew that the expected Messiah had come and that Christ was born, for it had been foretold to the people that Jesus Christ, the Son of God, would be born in Bethlehem, the town of David.

And the man rejoiced and was exceedingly joyful at the fulfilment of the long awaited prophecy and so he went to the stable and worshipped the new Christ, who lay in a cradle made from the manger of the horses.

It is because of this that Bride is called *Banchuideachaidh Moire*, 'the Aid-Woman of Mary', while others call her *Muime Chriosda*, 'Foster-Mother of Christ'. Christ himself is called *Dalta Bhríde*, 'the Foster-Son of Bride'. (CG §70, n.)

A Scottish tale accounts for how Brigid came to be present in Bethlehem:

Bride was set adrift in a basket as a helpless infant, and eventually floated ashore in a place where Druids dwelt. They found her and brought her up, and she remained happily with them until one day she was summoned by a white dove who guided her through a grove of hawthorn trees to a desert. She crossed this and arrived at Bethlehem where she assisted at the birth of the Divine Child and on his forehead she placed three drops of water. *(CG §217, n.)*

Still another version says that Bride was borne off to Bethlehem by angels from the isle of Iona, an important center of Celtic Christianity. Bride was said to have been brought as a child to Iona, where she was raised by Druids. On Iona she lived the simple life of a shepherdess, protected from chilly winds by the warm cloak she had woven with her own hands from the fleece of her flock. One night, angels appeared in Iona and told her she was needed in Bethlehem, whereupon they carried her to the far-away stable to assist in the birth. When she had delivered the Christ Child, she wrapped him in her own warm cloak. This tradition is the basis of a painting titled "St Bride Carried by Angels" by the early twentieth-century Scottish symbolist artist John Duncan. The richly colored canvas depicts two magnificently robed and haloed angels conveying a sleeping Brigid over Hebridean waters. A tiny silhouette of Iona Abbey, just visible in the lower right-hand corner of the frame, is a subtle tribute to Iona's role as a cradle of Celtic Christianity.

Some accounts say that besides delivering the infant Messiah, Bride served as his wet nurse and foster mother. In these stories, the Gaelic imagination is marvelously untroubled by the fact that Mary and Bride lived half a world and hundreds of years apart. Yet the stories are so engaging that the listener is inclined to forget the historic impossibilities. The imaginative premise that Bride could have been in the stable in Bethlehem to deliver the Christ Child, wrap him in her own cloak, and even nurse him at her own breast makes her role in bringing Christianity into the Gaelic world vivid and accessible. By weaving into the life of a native saint the Mother Goddess's protection of pregnant and nursing women and the spiritual nurture of

Druids, these richly imagined stories have created a foundation myth for Celtic Christianity.

The fertile Gaelic imagination has further elaborated the close ties between Bride and Mary through stories explaining the conjunction of their feast days in February. This period midway between the winter solstice and the vernal equinox is a time when the purification and fertility brought by the Divine Feminine is celebrated in many cultures. Brigid and Mary share the season with many goddesses, including the Egyptian goddess Nut, the Yoruba Orisha Oya, Greek Aphrodite, and Roman Vesta. But in the minds of the Gaels, Brigid's feast day on February 1 preceding Mary's festival of Candlemas on February 2 required some explanation.

The two festivals were originally unrelated. As one of the four Celtic festivals linked with the agricultural cycle, Brigid's Imbolc had been fixed by tradition long before Mary arrived on the scene. Mary's feast day had been independently established by the Church on Feb. 2 through a combination of scriptural tradition and simple arithmetical calculation. St. Luke's gospel says that Mary presented the infant Jesus in the temple in accordance with Mosaic law's requirement that a woman who had given birth to a son appear in the temple to be purified forty days after his birth. Forty days after December 25, the accepted birthdate of Jesus, is February 2, hence that became Mary's festival of Candlemas. The storytellers' explanations were much more imaginative. They claimed that Brigid's festival preceded Mary's because Brigid helped Mary out of a jam. They don't agree on the details of the emergency, but they concur that Brigid's strategy for helping Mary involved creating a distraction with lighted candles.

An Irish version of the story says that Brigid rescued the Holy Family when they ran into a roadblock on their flight into Egypt:

> When Mary and the Christ Child were fleeing into Egypt from King Herod, they found the road blocked by a party of soldiers, and Mary did not know what to do. Just then Brigid came along and offered to distract the soldiers from the fugitives. She did this by placing on her head a bright head-dress with lighted candles attached to it. She approached the soldiers, who were so amazed and intrigued by this strange sight, that they did not notice Mary and Jesus slip by. In thanks for the help Mary told Brigid that henceforth Brigid's feast would come one day before her own.

Other versions locate Brigid's intervention at the temple in Jerusalem during Mary's visit there:

> When Mary took the infant Jesus to the temple for the first time she found great crowds before it. However, Mary, being very diffident, dared not push her way through the crowds, so Brigid, who happened to be there, said she would help Mary by distracting the crowds. She then got some candles and placed them in her head-dress, causing the crowd to press round Brigid to see the strange sight of a young girl wearing a crown of lighted candles, thereby enabling Mary to slip into the temple. In thanks for this kindness Mary decreed that the feast day of Saint Brigid should be celebrated on the day before that of the Purification and the Candles.

A Hebridean version of the story includes candles but leaves out the headdress:

As the night was dark when the Virgin Mary went to the temple for purification, Brigid walked before her carrying a lighted candle in each hand and although a very strong wind was blowing they did not go out. For this kindness Mary said that Brigid's feast day should come one day before her own, which is why the saint is sometimes referred to in Scottish Gaelic as *Bhríde nan Coinnlean*—'Bride of the Candles.' (CG §70, n.)

Another Scottish version of the story adds an agricultural twist by replacing the candles with a harrow, a heavy rakelike farm tool with sharp points used for breaking up clods. This account says that when Brigid placed a harrow on her head, its upward-facing points magically became lighted candles, crowning Brigid with flames and creating a distracting sensation among the crowd.

### Foster Mother of Jesus

According to Hebridean legend, Bride's assistance to Mary did not end with delivering her child in a stable and using candles to manage troublesome soldiers, intimidating crowds, or fickle winds. Bride became a second parent to Jesus by serving as his foster mother. In the Celtic world, foster parentage was far more significant than such a relationship implies today. The practice of entrusting young children to the care of another family to be reared and educated was deeply implanted in Celtic culture. Irish mythology attests that fosterage formed exceptionally strong bonds among child, foster parents, and siblings. A shared history of fosterage lends tragic poignance to the climax of the *Cattle Raid of Cooley*, for example, when the hero Cu Chulainn is forced to fight his beloved foster brother, Ferdiad, to the death. The proverb "Blood to the twentieth, fostership to the hundredth degree" attests that the strength of foster bonds often surpassed those with the birth family. In a culture where foster relationships could forge bonds even stronger than blood, Bride's epithet "Foster Mother of Christ" implies equality with Mary as a co-mother to Jesus.

According to stories in *Carmina Gadelica*, Bride and Mary, in the way of mothers everywhere, liked to keep tabs on their boy. Their way of checking up on Jesus used a Druidic practice of augury called *frith*, which consisted of forming a tube with the left hand and peering through it like a telescope to see things at a far distance. One occasion when they used this technique was when twelve-year-old Jesus became separated from his parents during his first visit to the temple in Jerusalem. The story says that Mary looked through her imaginary telescope and saw Jesus sitting in the temple, conversing with the learned elders. Another time when Mary asked Brigid to help her find Jesus, Brigid "made a pipe within her palms" and saw him sitting beside a well, teaching.

> The augury Brigit made for her Foster-son, She
> made a pipe within her palms:
> 'I see the Foster-son by the well's side,
> Teaching the people assuredly.

I set the augury towards the well,
And truly that was righteous work,
The King of kings teaching the people,
Yonder I see Christ assuredly.' *(CG, § 539)*

An interesting detail of the story that Brigid located Jesus teaching at the well by peering through her imaginary telescope is that Brigid is in this instance given a husband; he is identified as the man who brought Jesus the water to wash the feet of his disciples. *(CG, § 537, n.)*

## Protection from All Ills

The oral material Alexander Carmichael collected in his many years of travel throughout the Hebrides offers glimpses of a culture in which sanctity was interwoven with the endless hard labor of farming, animal husbandry, fishing, and weaving. One woman recalled the rigors of her childhood:

> My mother was always at work, by day helping my father on the croft, and by night at wool and at spinning, at night clothes and at day clothes for the family. My mother would be beseeching us to be careful in everything, to put value on time and to eschew idleness; that a night was coming in which no work could be done. . . . If we were dilatory in putting on our clothes, and made an excuse for our prayers, my mother would say that God regarded heart and not speech, the mind and not the manner; and that we might clothe our souls with grace while clothing our bodies with raiment. (CG, § 222, n.)

This attitude that any activity could be sanctified with prayer was reflected in the existence of special prayers for all tasks and all seasons: milking the cows; making the bed; washing one's face; blessing the seed for planting; preparing the loom for weaving; blessing the cattle when they are turned out to graze; banking the household fire for the night and rekindling it in the morning; or warding off illness and evil. The prayers, poems, blessings, and charms included in *Carmina* show how Hebrideans made every task of daily life a small ritual of thanksgiving and praise.

A charming example of this sanctification of daily chores was the milking croons milkmaids sang to their cows. Hebridean cows were said to be so fond of music they refused to be milked unless their milkmaids sang to them, and the names of Mary and Bride were often linked in their songs:

Come, Mary Virgin, to my cow,
Come, great Bride, the beauteous,
Come, thou milkmaid of Jesus Christ,
And place thine arms beneath my cow.
Ho my heifer, ho my gentle heifer. (CG, § 99)

Milkmaids also gave the four teats of their cows individual names, claiming that each of the four teats had special qualities:

Teat of Mary,
Teat of Brigid,
Teat of Michael,
Teat of God. (*CG, §373*)

The Brigid teat was said to give butter.

The names of Mary and Bride were frequently invoked for protection of the sheep and cattle on which the life of the people depended:

> I will place this flock before me,
> As I was ordained of the King of the world,
> Bride to keep them, to watch them, to tend them,
> On ben, on glen, on plain.
> Bride to keep them, to watch them, to tend them,
> On ben, on glen, on plain.
> Arise, thou Bride the gentle, the fair,
> Take thou thy lint, thy comb, and thy hair,
> Since thou to them madest the noble charm,
> To keep them from straying, to save them from harm,
> Since thou to them madest the noble charm,
> To keep them from straying, to save them from harm.
>
> From rocks, from drifts, from streams,
> From crooked passes, from destructive pits,
> From the straight arrows of the slender ban-shee,
> From the heart of envy, from the eye of evil,
> From the straight arrows of the slender ban-shee,
> From the heart of envy, from the eye of evil.
>
> Mary Mother, tend thou the offspring, all,
> Bride of the fair palms, guard thou my flocks,
> Kindly Columba, thou saint of many powers,
> Encompass thou the breeding cows,
> bestow on me herds,
> Kindly Columba, thou saint of many powers,
> Encompass thou the breeding cows,
> bestow on me herds. *(CG, § 101)*

Bride and Mary were also routinely invoked in petitions for the protection of people in the midst of the hardships and dangers of Hebridean life. This prayer, *The Genealogy of Bride,* is an abbreviated version of a lengthier prayer called *Womanhood of Brigit* or *Praises of Brigit,* that was considered an all-purpose defense against personal danger.

> Every day and night
> That I say the genealogy of Bride,
> I shall not be killed, I shall not be harried,
> I shall not be put in cell, I shall not be wounded,
> Neither shall Christ leave me in forgetfulness.
>
> No fire, no sun, no moon shall burn me,
> No lake, no water, nor sea shall drown me,
> No arrow of fairy nor dart of fay shall wound me,
> And I under the protection of my Holy Mary,
> And my gentle foster-mother is my beloved Bride.
> *(CG,* § 264)

It is not surprising given her many connections with fire that Brigid was also the recipient of prayers for the tending of the household hearth. In the Hebrides, where peat was the principal fuel, the fire was damped, or "smoored," at bedtime so that it could easily be rekindled in the morning. Carmichael characterizes smooring as a "ceremony . . . performed with loving care." It was accompanied by a prayer for protection of the household as all prepared for sleep:

> I will smoor the hearth
> As Brigit the Foster-mother would smoor.

The Foster-mother's holy name
Be on the hearth, be on the herd,
Be on the household all. *(CG,* § 323)

Early the next morning before anyone else was up, the woman of the house would revive the banked fire as she offered a prayer for her household:

I will raise the hearth-fire
As Mary would.
The encirclement of Bride and of Mary
On the fire, and on the floor,
And on the household all.
Who are they on the bare floor?
John and Peter and Paul.
Who are they by my bed?
The lovely Bride and her Fosterling.
Who are those watching over my sleep?
The fair loving Mary and her Lamb.
Who is that anear me?
The King of the sun, He himself it is.
Who is that at the back of my head?
The Son of Life without beginning, without time.
*(CG,* §83)

By the late nineteenth century when Carmichael was collecting the oral treasures he preserved in *Carmina Gadelica,* the traditional way of life so long protected by the geographic isolation of the Hebrides was swiftly passing away. Still, in what remains of this material we get a picture of Bride's important roles—as trustworthy midwife, protector from life's dangers, and sanctifier of the humblest occasions of daily life. Carmichael's decades of collecting oral material throughout the Hebrides led him to conclude that "there were several Brides, Christian and pre-Christian, whose personalities have become confused in the course of centuries—the attributes of all being now popularly ascribed to one. Bride is said to preside over fire, over art, over all beauty. . . . She is the Mary and the Juno of the Gael." (*CG*, §70, n.)

# Chapter Five
# Bringer of Spring

Sant Ffraid, February saint,
unfreezer, unlooser, giver, saint of the farms,
bless now the year's work starting
with the hard ice melting!
. . .
Bride, goddess, bring now
the breaking, the slaking,
the flowing, the growing!
                    Ruth Bidgood, "Hymn to Sant Ffraid"


Imbolc, or *Feile Bride,* celebrated Brigid's role as the bringer of beneficent seasonal change. The beginning of February was the time when the first signs of hope began to dispel the tedium of long winter months of forced inactivity, with little fresh food available. A traditional poem celebrates Brigid's role as the bringer of welcome signs of spring:

Bride put her finger in the river
on the Feast Day of Bride,
and away went the hatching mother of the cold.
And she bathed her palms in the river
on the Feast Day of Patrick
and away went the conception
of the mother of cold. *(CG,* §70, n.)

*Cormac's Glossary* offers two alternative names for Brigid's festival, both connected with the lambing season: *Imbolc,* meaning "in the belly," and *Oimelc,* meaning "ewe's milk." In the tale *Tochmarc Emire* ("The Wooing of Emer") Imbolc is called "the time when the ewes are milked at spring's beginning." The fat-rich milk of ewes was the first fresh food farm families could add to the monotonous diet of the long winter months. The lambing season was accompanied by signs of awakening nature, especially the blooming of early flowers and the nesting of birds:

> On the Feast Day of beautiful Bride,
> The flocks are counted on the moor,
> The raven goes to prepare the nest,
> And again goes the rook. (*CG,* §70, n.)

Domestic fowl, too, were nesting. An Irish oral history testifies: "Eggs were put down to hatch on St. Brigid's Day if there was a broody hen to be got, as tradition had it that anything that started its growth on that day would prove 100% fertile. There is nothing in the water or on the ground that is not thinking of propagating by the Feast of St. Brigid."[1]

A traditional poem enumerates some of the signs of spring:

> The Day of Bride, the birthday of Spring,
> The serpent emerges from the knoll,
> 'Three-years-olds' is applied to heifers,
> [Ponies] are taken to the fields. (*CG,* §70, n.)

The emergence of the serpent from the knoll was a specific sign looked for by Scottish farmers. On Bride's Day, farmers would gather expectantly at the hole of the hibernating adder to look for signs of activity. When adders came out of their winter burrows, it was an indication that the soil was warming and was therefore ready to be plowed and planted. To coax the serpent from its burrow, they would recite charms, often including a promise that if the snake came out, it would not be harmed.

> Early on Bride's morn
> The serpent shall come from the hole;
> I will not molest the serpent,
> Nor will the serpent molest me.

Since it was reckoned bad luck to use the creature's name, the serpent was referred to as "the Noble Queen" or "Daughter of Ivor."

> On the day of Bride of the white hills
> The noble queen will come from the knoll;
> I will not molest the noble queen,
> Nor will the noble queen molest me

> ~

> The Feast Day of Bride
> The Daughter of Ivor shall come from the knoll,
> I will not touch the daughter of Ivor,
> Nor shall she harm me. (*CG*, §70, n.)

The assurance of mutual harmlessness in these Scottish charms is shared by incantations from India and China that tempt serpents or dragons who sleep all winter and awaken in the spring. Here is a Chinese version of the charm:

If we offer a deprecatory service to them
They will leave their abodes;
If we do not seek the dragons
They will not seek us.

This promise of a reciprocal covenant with the powers of nature contains overtones of primal associations of dragons and serpents with the Mother Goddess.

## Bride of the Isles

The particular benefits Brigid brought with spring varied according to geography. Throughout Ireland as well as much of Scotland, Brigid was seen as the protector of the welfare of farming people and their herds and flocks. Residents of coastal areas awaited her as the bringer of beneficial tides and bountiful harvests from the sea. In the Hebrides and the Orkneys and other places where life depended on the combined produce of sea and land, she was called "Bride of the Isles" or "Brigid of the Shores." Fiona MacLeod describes the bounty associated with the favorable omen of hearing the oystercatcher's call on Bride's Day:

> Fisherfolk on the shores of the west and on the far isles have gladdened at the first prolonged repetitive whistle of the oyster opener, for its advent means that the hosts of the good fish are moving towards the welcoming coasts once more, that the wind of the south is unloosened, that greenness will creep to the grass, that birds will seek the bushes, that song will come to them, and that everywhere a new gladness will be abroad. By these signs is St. Briget of the Shores known.[2]

In the Isles, Brigid's Day signaled the return of the spring tides that brought shoals of fish to coastal waters and marked the beginning of the fishing season. In the Hebridean island of Barra, it was formerly customary to apportion fishing banks on Bride's Day. After a church service dedicated to the blessings bestowed by St. Bride, the men would gather at the church door to cast lots for the fishing banks. (CG, §70, n.) People in living in coastal areas today still look forward to the extra-low spring tide nearest St. Brigid's Day as an opportunity to collect shellfish and gather the seaweed they use to fertilize their crops.[3]

The island of South Uist has a picturesque tradition that Brigid comes ashore each spring in a goddesslike pose, bearing an oystercatcher on each upraised wrist. Brigid's association with these birds comes from the birds' call of "Gilly-Breed, Gilly-Breed, Gilly-Breed," which is a homophone for "Gille-Bhride," or "Servant of Bride." A more imaginative explanation comes from folklore that says that Brigid adopted the species out of gratitude for a service the birds did for her or her foster son, Jesus. One such story says that oystercatchers became Brigid's servants after they hid the boy Jesus from nefarious pursuers who were chasing him along the beach.

### Brigid and the Cailleach

Scottish myth portrays the annual struggle between winter and spring as a war between Brigid and her rival, the Cailleach Bheara. The fierce Cailleach comes into power in autumn as the days shorten and the sun is low in the skies, bringing cold, wind, and tempests. In the Hebrides, she ushers in winter at Samhain by washing her big plaid in the whirlpool of Corryvreckan ("Cauldron of the Plaid") between the islands of Jura and Scarba. The washing is preceded by the roar of a tempest that can be heard for twenty miles for three days before the cauldron begins to boil. When the washing is over, the colorful plaid of Scotland's hills has turned pure white with snowfall.

The Cailleach's power to impose winter is assisted by her *slachdan*, a white magic wand or hammer, which turns water to ice and prevents growth anywhere she throws it. The fact that no grass grows under the holly tree is explained as the result of the Cailleach's fury at the sight of the grass and sun of early spring. She is said to have flung her wand under a holly tree and retreated, cursing the holly forever.

One legend says that in winter, the Cailleach keeps the beautiful maiden Bride imprisoned in the fastness of Ben Nevis, the highest peak in the British Isles. The Cailleach's son Angus falls in love with the maiden, and the young couple elope at the end of winter, but the Cailleach raises terrible storms to keep them apart. Despite the many obstacles to their happiness she creates by her persistent efforts to revive winter, Angus and Bride finally celebrate their union on the Day of Bride.

One tradition about the Cailleach resonates with the Groundhog Day lore familiar to North Americans. It is said that on Bride's Day the Cailleach gathers her firewood for the rest of the winter. A bright, sunny day that allows her to gather plenty of firewood is a sign that winter is going to last several weeks longer. But foul weather on Bride's Day indicates that the Cailleach is still asleep. She will soon run out of firewood, meaning that winter is almost over.

One of the earliest Scottish legends of the coming of spring depicts Bride and the Cailleach not as rivals but as polarities of a single nature goddess:

On the Eve of Bride, the Cailleach repairs to the Isle of Youth, in whose woods lies the miraculous Well of Youth. There, at the first glimmer of dawn, before any bird has sung or any dog barked, she drinks of the water that bubbles from a crevice of the rock. The water of the well renews her youth and she emerges as Bride, the fair young goddess, the touch of whose wand turns dun grass to vivid green, starred with the white and yellow flowers of spring.

## The Celebration of Brigid's Feast

Three of the traditional Celtic festivals that marked the agricultural cycle were celebrated in boisterous regional gatherings featuring bonfires, feasting, and revelry. In contrast, Imbolc was a much quieter domestic celebration. Brigid's Eve was observed in the home with a ritual meal and simple, homemade ceremonial items fabricated from the limited resources at hand, such as straw left from the last season's harvest. While customs varied from place to place, the celebrations show that legends of the Christian saint were entwined with ancient pre-Christian ritual practices and beliefs about the Divine Feminine.

The most challenging task for every householder preparing for Brigid's arrival was to procure a supply of butter, which by late January was a very scarce commodity. Folk wisdom held that a cow's milk went up into her horns from Christmas to Brigid's Day. A traditional rhyme attests the calamity of being without butter for Brigid's Feast:

Samhain Eve without food,
Christmas Night without bread,
St. Brigid's Eve without butter,
That is a sorry complaint.

Every household would scrimp to ensure that there would be butter for the celebratory meal on the eve of Brigid's Day. If anyone complained about the scarcity of milk in January, the old people would say, "It won't be scarce very long now as St. Brigid and her white cow will be coming round soon."[4]

Brigid's protection was especially coveted for cows and their vulnerable newborn calves. Her protection of the human residents of the household focused on the miraculous powers of her famous cloak. Each household collected some of this protective power by means of a piece of fabric called the *Brat Bríde* or "Brigid's Cloak." A garment or piece of cloth would be left on a windowsill, fence, or tree branch to be blessed by St. Brigid during the night when she passed by. The next day the *Brat Bríde* would be divided among the females in the household to confer Brigid's blessing, fertility, and healing throughout the year. Pieces of the *brat* might be sewn into girls' clothes to guard them from misfortune and preserve their virginity.[5] The blending of Christian and pagan elements in Imbolc made for a paradox concerning the *brat*: The same talisman that protected the sexual purity of girls could also be used as a fertility aid to promote conception or ensure a safe delivery for women or cows.

The *Brat Bríde* tradition illustrates the inventiveness that went into the creation of ritual accessories from the scarce resources at hand. Any ordinary garment or piece of fabric could become a powerful talisman when it was imbued with Brigid's protection on Imbolc Eve. At the time of year when food was scarcest, the everyday fare of the farm table could be transformed into a ritual "feast" by the inclusion of precious butter along with the symbolic presence of St. Brigid at the dinner table. Straw left from the previous season's harvest was used to fabricate ritual accessories, which might include an effigy called a *Brídeog* ("Young Brigid" or "Brigid the Virgin"), a straw mattress known as *Leaba Bhride* ("Brigid's Bed"), a *Crios Bríde* ("Brigid's Girdle"), and St. Brigid crosses. Traditions about the fabrication of these accessories and how they were used varied from place to place, but these homely, handcrafted articles were universally believed to retain the *mana* of the feminine powers of fertility and protection.

In the Hebrides, it was customary for the *Brídeog* effigy to be fashioned by the girls of the community from the last sheaf of grain left from the previous year's harvest, which was called "The Cailleach." The *Brídeog* would be embellished with early-blooming flowers and seashells, with a crystal or bright shell placed over the heart. The girls, dressed in white and wearing their hair loose as a symbol of purity, would process from house to house, singing a song to Bride. Each household would be expected to give Bride a gift. The older women prepared a bed for the *Brídeog*, a *Lheaba Bride* ("Bed of Bride"). The image of Bride was reverently placed in it along with the *slachdan Bhride* ("the little wand of Bride"), a peeled white rod of sacred wood that resembled traditional Druid wands associated with prophecy, justice, and purity. *(CG, §70, n.)*

It was also traditional in the Hebrides for the nightly smooring of the fire to be performed with special care on Bride's Eve. In the morning, the family eagerly examined the ashes for marks of Bride's wand or a footprint indicating that she had visited in the night. Such marks were considered lucky signs that the coming year would bring an increase in family or livestock. If no marks were found in the ashes, it meant that Bride had been offended in some way. The family might try to make amends by burning incense and offering oblation, sometimes by burying a cockerel alive near the junction of three streams.[6] *(CG, §70, n.)*

A saint's festival that incorporated such practices as animal sacrifice and the charming of serpents seems to verify Sir James Fraser's summary of Brigid as "an old pagan goddess of fertility disguised in a threadbare Christian cloak." Celtic scholar Séamas Ó Catháin has identified many pagan elements in the ritual meal on the Eve of St. Brigid's Day. Ó Catháin sees the ritual meal as a symbolic dramatization of the sexual union that produces fertility. He describes the Irish version of the ritual beginning at the threshold with the verbal consent of the household members to participate in the ritual. The straw *Brídeog* would be brought inside to join the family for a meal that included butter and "poundies," or potatoes mashed with butter. This ritual foodstuff was produced by a vigorous churning or pounding action that mimicked sexual intercourse.

When the meal was finished, everyone in the household would join in the weaving of St. Brigid's crosses from straw or reed, talismans that would retain the fertility and protection the ritual meal had aroused. The next day the woven crosses could be used to confer blessings upon the family and their beasts and protect the house from fire. In some places, it was traditional to sprinkle the newly woven crosses with water from a well dedicated to St. Brigid before attaching them to the rafters of the house and outbuildings. In County Leitrim, it was customary for the head of the household to carry a cross around to every window and door, saying at each entrance, "St. Brigid save us from all fever, famine and fire," then affixing the cross over the kitchen door.[7] A cross might be put into a basket of seed potatoes to transmit blessings to the new crop. St. Brigid Crosses could also be used as fertility charms, as they were in County Mayo, where newly married couples might find under their mattress a straw cross placed there by a mother or mother-in-law to ensure the generation of children.

In addition to these domestic rites, Imbolc was observed in the community by processions of children or young people who carried a ritual item from house to house, offering blessings in exchange for small gifts. In Ireland, the *Brídeog* procession consisted of guising youths carrying an effigy of Brigid from door to door. They would offer entertainment and prayers at each household, then ask for "something for the *Brídeog*," usually a gift of bread or butter that would serve as part of a celebratory "feast" for the mummers at the end of the evening.[8]

Irish celebrations sometimes included a plaited straw loop called a *Crios Bríde,* or "Brigid's Girdle," carried from house to house by a troupe of boys. The bearers offered householders the opportunity of gaining health and good fortune by passing through Brigid's Girdle in exchange for a small reward such as an egg or a penny. The benefits conferred by the *Crios Bríde* were based on the supposed healing powers of St. Brigid's belt. The *Life of St Brigid* relates this tale:

A certain woman came to Brigid seeking alms and the saint offered to give her either her cloak or a calf that had recently been presented to her. The woman, however, explained that such gifts would be useless to her as robbers whom she would meet in her travels would take them from her. The saint then told her she had heard that illness was rife in her native district and gave her the belt she was wearing, telling her that the water in which it was dipped would cure the invalids and that she would receive food and clothing for curing them.[9]

The *Crios Bride* ceremony was also consistent with pagan beliefs that passing through a hole in certain stones could confer healing.

Emerging from the *Crios Bríde* was a symbolic rebirth from the womb of the goddess that was supposed to bring health and good fortune. Those who accepted the *Crios Bríde* invitation would pass through the braided loop three times, emerging right foot forward and kissing the girdle to ensure health and good fortune, while the boys chanted:

> The Girdle, the Girdle of Brigid, my Girdle,
> The Girdle of the four crosses,
> Mary entered it,
> Brigid emerged from it;
> If you be improved today,
> May you be seven times better
> A year from today.[10]

A householder who refused the girdle ritual or failed to give the bearers a small reward, however, would earn a curse:

> The Girdle of Brigid is my Girdle,
> The Girdle of the four crosses.
> The person who will not give me a penny
> May the Devil break his foot.

Little of Imbolc survives in modern times, but the Brigid's Girdle ritual has found a place in the poetry of Seamus Heaney, who recalled some of the Imbolc traditions were still observed in Ireland during his childhood. Heaney perceptively captures the archetypal experience of rebirth embedded within the customs and superstitions attached to Imbolc:

> On St. Brigid's Day the new life could be entered
> By going through her girdle of straw rope:
> The proper way for men was right leg first,
>
> Then right arm and right shoulder, head, then left
> Shoulder, arm and leg. Women drew it down
> Over the body and stepped out of it.
>
> The open they came into by these moves
> Stood opener, hoops came off the world,
> They could feel the February air
>
> Still soft above their heads and imagine
> The limp rope fray and flare like wind-borne gleanings
> Or an unhindered goldfinch over ploughland.[11]

Most customs of St. Brigid's Day have fallen away, but love for Brigid has never ceased to burn brightly in the Gaelic soul. A traditional song, "Gabhaim Molta Bride" ("I Praise Brigid"), attests that she remains an eternal icon of the return of spring:

> I praise Brigid
> Beloved in Ireland
> Beloved in all countries
> Let us all praise her.

The bright torch of Leinster
Shining throughout the country,
The pride of Irish youth,
The pride of our gentle women.
The house of winter is very dark,
Cutting with its sharpness,
But on Brigid's Day
Spring is near to Ireland.

PART TWO

# The Exile
# of the Goddess
# &
# The Unbalancing
# of Western
# Civilization

# Chapter Six
# The Dragonslayers
# and the Exile of the Goddess

Success to bold St. Patrick's fist,
He was a saint so clever,
He gave the snakes and toads a twist,
And banished them forever!
                              Irish toast

[Marduk] placed his feet on the lower parts of
Tia-mat
And with his merciless club smashed her skull.
He severed her arteries
And let the North wind bear up (her blood) to
give the news.
His fathers saw it and were glad and exulted;
They brought gifts and presents to him.
                    *Enuma Elish*, 2nd millennium B.C.E.

We have seen that the archetypal Divine Feminine
energies embodied in Brigid survive in places, yet apart
from isolated Celtic enclaves, few parts of the civilized West
recognize this power of the feminine. Why is this so? If we

ever knew of the sacred dance of Yang and Yin or Shiva and Shakti depicted in Eastern mythologies, what has become of that perception? Our mythology hints that the feminine has been deliberately exiled so that the masculine could lay claim to the entire dance.

Let's begin with St. Brigid's colleague, St. Patrick, probably the most popular of all the Irish saints. After all, what's not to like about a clever fellow who used a shamrock to introduce Christianity to Ireland, then drove out all the snakes? If we dig into the legends a bit, though, we find that his reputation is just a wee bit inflated. It is true that Patrick contributed significantly to planting Christianity in the island where he was once an enslaved captive, but in fact Christianity already had a foothold in Ireland before he returned there to missionize the Irish, so he doesn't deserve all the credit. The bit about the expulsion of snakes, alas, is charming but complete blarney. Ireland has never had snakes since the submersion of the land bridge that united the island to larger land masses about 20,000 years ago. But blarney or not, Patrick's reputed snake banishing is the part of his legend I want to talk about.

On one level the St. Patrick snake banishing legend is a classic "just-so story," a fanciful folk explanation of a local phenomenon.

Q: "Why aren't there any snakes in Ireland?"

A: "Because St. Patrick drove them all into the sea."

A similar just-so story credits St. Columba with ridding Iona of snakes and toads. These fanciful tales about reptile-ousting saints are amusing, but they can be read as more than entertainment. On a mythological level, the legend that Patrick expelled the snakes from Ireland can be interpreted as a celebration of Christianity's victory over paganism. The snakes stand for Satan along with the chaos and evil that Christianity sought to banish from Celtic lands. Similar legends from Scotland and England represent this triumph through stories of St. George and St. Michael, who slew dragons that embodied chaos and evil.

Yet there was a time when the serpents and dragons that represent chaos and evil in Christian legends symbolized the Mother Goddess, who was worshiped as the Source of life. Christianity did not invent the demonization of serpents and dragons or the banishment of the Goddess. That process had been going on for more than two thousand years before Christianity came on the scene. Triumphant Christian warrior-saints were simply the latest champions in a long campaign. To understand how the Great Goddess became so thoroughly demonized that even the destruction of her symbols was cause for celebration, we have to look back into Western mythology before the Christian era.

## The Defeat of the Goddess

In the mid-nineteenth century, archaeologists investigating the ruins of the library of Ashurbanipal in the ancient city of Nineveh discovered thousands of clay cuneiform tablets that had been preserved by having been burned in a fire. One of the greatest discoveries in that vast treasure trove was the Babylonian *Enuma Elish,* a mythic text written down ca. 1200 B.C.E. It was the very first creation myth ever to be preserved in writing.

The story is framed as a family feud with dire consequences. The young gods, sons of Tiamat, the primordial goddess of the sea who gave birth to the world, and Apsu, the god of fresh waters, are sick and tired of Tiamat's authority. They would like nothing more than to overthrow her, but they're afraid of the formidable powers of their mother, who appears in the form of a terrible sea serpent. Caught fast between ambition and self-pity, the young gods whine, "Nowhere is there a god who will attack Tiamat. He would not escape from Tiamat's presence with his life." Enter their brother Marduk, the sun god. In the midst of this mewling discontent, he steps up and volunteers to take Tiamat on in combat. All his cowardly brothers have to do is agree that if he wins, he can be king of Babylon. The brothers are only too glad to take Marduk up on his offer to be their champion.

Marduk's confrontation with Tiamat warms up with a little trash talk, but it quickly devolves into brutal, no-holds-barred combat. At first, Tiamat appears to have the upper hand, but Marduk outmaneuvers her by using the winds that are his playthings to distend her belly, then firing an arrow into her mouth, rupturing her stomach and piercing her heart. After that, he splits her body in half "like a dried fish" and places one half on high to become the heavens and the other below to be the earth. He then methodically dismembers her and creates the world from the parts of her body. Her buttocks become the mountains, and her breasts become the foothills. He uses her pubic mound to support the sky. The tears that flow from Tiamat's eyes become the waters of the Tigris and Euphrates rivers. He goes on to create mountains, earth, clouds, wind, and mists, to organize the constellations, make the moon appear, and establish the seasons.[1] This story of Marduk's murder and dismemberment of his mother became the foundation myth of Babylon, where it was publicly recited as part of the New Year's festival every spring for a thousand years.[2]

*Enuma Elish* was groundbreaking in that it turned previous oral creation myths upside down. Prior to the second millennium B.C.E., the oral mythology of the Ancient Near East had depicted Creation as the result of procreation by a powerful mother goddess. It was a story of birth-giving. When the Babylonian version was written down, the procreative act of a mother goddess was changed into an act of fabrication by male deities. In *Enuma Elish*, the creation story became an account of the murder and mutilation of the mother goddess Tiamat by her sons, who use the parts of her body to construct the world.

The murder of the Mother Goddess represents a development in consciousness whereby humans began to withdraw their projections of divinity away from the Great Mother and identify instead with the ascendent symbol of the sun god. Of this transition, Marion Woodman and Elinor Dickinson write that nature became, instead of the source of power, "something to be controlled and dominated. In an odd reversal of roles, nature was now pressed into the service of man. Power came to be perceived as deriving from strength. Virtually unchanged since its inception, this paradigm has dominated Western civilization down to the present."[3]

This great psychic change went along with the immense surge of cultural innovation in the Ancient Near East that constituted the beginning of Western civilization. The construction of great walled cities, the building of empires, and an explosion of innovation and learning were facilitated by a splitting apart of masculine and feminine energies that allowed masculine energies to take the lead.

In *The Alphabet Versus the Goddess: The Conflict Between Word and Image,* Leonard Shlain argues persuasively that the emergence of alphabetic writing was a primary means by which the demise of the goddess was achieved. In his view, the mental operations involved in literacy, whereby information is broken into small bits through the left-brain functions of separation, abstraction, and linear sequencing, disrupt the collaboration of the cerebral hemispheres and cause actual physiological changes in the brain. The prevalence of literacy has resulted in a strong preference for the analytical functions of the left brain over the more integrative functions of the right brain. The upshot of the culture's heavy reliance on literacy has, as he puts it, given our civilization a strong "Yang thrust."

The great power literacy confers has made it the defining skill for being "civilized." Anyone who learns to crack the codes of alphabet, grammar, and syntax gains immense power in worldly transactions. Literacy makes it possible to transmit written information across town or across time. A literate person can use the letters of the alphabet to create anything from a grocery list to a weather forecast, a philosophy, an advertising slogan, a love note, or the complete works of Shakespeare. The related ability to analyze and synthesize has improved human life in ways too numerous to count. It has greatly eased the labor of everyday life, given us advantages over disease, and presented us with penicillin, air conditioning, and space travel.

Yet as Sophocles observed, "Nothing vast enters the life of mortals without a curse." The gift to humankind that undergirded the development of science, literature, government, and the many marvels of the modern world also has a shadow side. Claude Lévi-Strauss puts it this way: "The only phenomenon which, always and in all parts of the world, seems to be linked with the appearance of writing . . . is the establishment of hierarchical societies, consisting of masters and slaves, where one part of the population is made to work for the other part."[4] The dark side of literacy is that it facilitates the creation of hierarchical social structures. Thus, alongside its many gifts, literacy supports the creation of patriarchal, hierarchical social structures that have been used to justify the institution of slavery and defined women as property that could be owned and exchanged by men. Even today, a bride who elects to be "given" in marriage by her father and vows to obey her husband is honoring the legacy of ancient patriarchal laws. In short, the development of writing that made civilized life possible and enhanced the status of certain classes of people has also dramatically limited the scope of life for others.

The ascendency of masculine energies enabled by alphabetic writing and revised mythology was assisted by a third innovation: the development of written law codes. The best-known example of an Ancient Near Eastern law code is the Code of Hammurabi, which bears the name of the eighteenth-century B.C.E. king who brought all of Mesopotamia under Babylonian control. Like the oral myths that were extensively revised in their written versions, oral laws underwent major changes as they were being written down. Whereas oral laws had leaned toward restorative justice by prescribing compensation for victims of crime, the written law codes emphasized retribution and punishment. Hammurabi's Code, for example, included the famous prescription of "an eye for an eye," the *lex talionis*. Law codes also reflected social hierarchies by making the severity of criminal penalties vary according to the gender and social class of both lawbreaker and victim. The written laws were literally "carved in stone." Hammurabi had his 282 laws inscribed on a massive black diorite stele topped with a bas-relief depiction of the king receiving the law from the sun god. The immense stone was placed in a public location in Babylon, and copies were distributed throughout the kingdom. Hammurabi meant for all the world to see the written laws that maintained order over chaos and held the kingdom together.

## Monotheism and the Banishment of the Goddess

By the mid-nineteenth century when the *Enuma Elish* tablets were discovered, the overthrow of the Goddess disclosed in the myth was hardly headline news. The triumph of masculine over feminine had by then been part of Western religious mythology for more than three thousand years. The sacred scriptures in whose pages it had been handed down proclaimed as divine revelation that the singular, masculine, omnipotent God wills a human society that includes hierarchy and patriarchy.

Although the annihilation of the Goddess was not newsworthy, certain discoveries in Ashurburnipal's library did cause shock waves in biblical studies. The new discoveries revealed that far from constituting unique revelations, as had long been assumed, many of the stories in the Hebrew Scriptures were shared with other cultures of the Ancient Near East. One of the most important newly discovered documents, for example, the *Epic of Gilgamesh*, contained the tale of one Utnapishtim, who was divinely commissioned to build a great ship to save animals and a handful of people from the great flood that would destroy life on earth. Even parallels to the killing of the Mother Goddess Tiamat could be recognized in the oldest passages in Hebrew scripture, two Psalms praising YHWH for gaining dominion over the universe by killing primal sea serpents alternatively named either Leviathan (Ps. 74) or Rahab (Ps. 89).

But the Hebrew Scriptures also differed from the common pool of Ancient Near Eastern mythologies in important ways. The most significant departure was a relocation of the Divine essence expressed through a pantheon of deities into YHWH, a single, masculine god. The means through which this was done made use of the three Bronze Age innovations that favor left brain abstraction: revised mythology, law codes, and alphabetic writing.[5] All three are used to create the foundation myth of Yahwism, the giving of the law at Mount Sinai. That event reifies the sovereignty of the one god through a written law code called a covenant.

The covenant inscribed on the tablets Moses brought down from Mount Sinai was not greatly different from other Ancient Near Eastern law codes in that it prohibited acts that threatened the orderly life of the community. Its main distinction is the affirmation of a singular deity. But the Sinai Code does contain a particular stipulation that is unique among codes of law: "You shall not make images of anything in heaven, earth, or the world below" (Exodus 20:4). This startling statement that comes second in the law code implies that the creation of material images is more threatening to the sovereignty of the deity and the integrity of the community than adultery, theft, covetousness, lying, or even murder.[6] From a modern understanding of neuroscience, the Second Commandment might be seen as a prohibition against the operation of the right brain.

The subsequent preaching of the Hebrew prophets indicates that the Sinai Code was far from universally successful in stemming the flow of divine feminine energies. Jeremiah describes his dismay at seeing entire families flouting the law by participating in the worship of the Queen of Heaven: "The children gather wood, the fathers light the fire, and the women knead the dough and make cakes of bread for the Queen of Heaven" (Jeremiah 7:18). He also reports protests by the men of Israel that "ever since we stopped burning incense to the Queen of Heaven and pouring out drink offerings to her, we have had nothing and have been perishing by sword and famine" (Jeremiah 44:18).

## The Greeks and the Banishment of the Goddess

The ethos of the West is the offspring of a fantastically improbable marriage between the austere, desert-bred monotheism of the Hebrews and the voluptuous poly-theism of Mediterranean Greeks. That two such dissimilar cultures could be amalgamated in any way is cause for wonder. Yet, the Hebrews and Greeks shared one characteristic that contributed to the exile of the Goddess: They were the first two societies that unreservedly embraced the alphabet and subsequently usurped the power of the feminine.[7]

Greek mythological heroes specialized in slaying serpents and dragons in exchange for wisdom or power. In return for slaying the she-snake Python that guarded the Delphic oracle, for example, the sun god Apollo was rewarded with the gift of foresight. Jason's quest for the solar trophy of the Golden Fleece required him to slay a dragon. Perseus beheaded the snake-haired feminine Gorgon. Heracles was still an infant when he strangled two giant snakes sent by a jealous Hera to dispatch him in his cradle.

It is the myth of Cadmus, the first Greek hero, that ties the conquest of the feminine directly to the introduction of the alphabet. Cadmus was a Phoenician prince whose sister, Europa, was abducted by Zeus in the guise of a bull. Europa's father, King Agenor of Tyre, sent his three sons abroad to search for his daughter, giving Cadmus the assignment of searching in Greece. After months of wandering through the land without finding Europa, he came to Delphi, believed to be the center of the world. There, Cadmus consulted the oracle for advice, but instead of telling him where to find Europa, she advised him to abandon his search for his sister and follow a cow with the mark of a half-moon on her flank until the creature fell down in exhaustion. He was then to sacrifice her on the spot and establish a city, for in that place he was destined to become a mighty king.

Cadmus took the oracle's advice. He abandoned his search for his sister and followed the cow. When the cow finally collapsed at a place called Thebes, Cadmus slit her throat as an offering to Athena and sent two of his men to fetch water from a nearby spring so that he could complete the preparation of the sacrifice. But the terrible water-dragon that guarded the spring killed his men, so Cadmus had to kill the dragon to avenge them before he could complete his sacrifice to Athena. Athena expressed her pleasure with his sacrifice by instructing Cadmus to pull the dragon's golden teeth, which were the source of its wisdom and power, and sow half the teeth in a nearby field. He followed Athena's instructions, and from each tooth sprang a fierce, fully armed warrior. The dragon's teeth represent the letters of the alphabet that Cadmus brought to Greece from his native Phoenicia, and the warriors that sprang from them signify the power of the alphabetic letters to tear reality into small bites, making possible the conquest of knowledge.[8]

The Greeks are, as far as we know, the only culture to lose the power of literacy then to regain it after an intervening dark age of 350 years. It was during the period when literacy returned to Greece, about 750 B.C.E., that oral mythology, including the epics of Homer, began to be written down. Just as the feminine suffered diminished status when Near Eastern mythology was recorded in writing, Greek goddesses lost power when oral myths were written down. The revised origin stories of Hera, Athena, and Aphrodite, for example, portray the goddesses being born entirely through masculine agency, without recourse to mothers or wombs. Aphrodite was conceived in the sea from the genitals of the Titan Uranus and born from the foam of the waves. Hera was "born" from the stomach of her father, Cronus. Athena gestated in Zeus's body after he swallowed her pregnant mother and was born from his brain fully grown and clad in battle armor.

Similarly misogynistic myths appear in another of the early written works, Hesiod's *Theogonis* (seventh to eighth century B.C.E.). When the Titan Prometheus defied the gods' order by giving fire to humankind, he was punished for his disobedience by being chained to a rock and having an eagle devour his liver each day. Humanity was also punished for receiving the forbidden divine fire. Their punishment was being sent Pandora, the first woman. Hesiod writes: "So women are a curse to mortal men—as Zeus ordained—partners in evil deeds. For fire's boon he made a second curse" *(Theogonis, 42)*. The smith god Hephaestus is commissioned to fabricate a woman who is given the name "Pandora," meaning "all gifted" or "all-giving," formerly an epithet of the Great Mother. The deities adorn her in finery and lavish on her the gifts of grace, beauty, cunning, and curiosity. Zeus then delivers her to humanity as an enticing but troublesome companion for men. She is given as a wife to Epimetheus, the brother of Prometheus, along with a mysterious jar, which she is strictly forbidden to open. But her inherent curiosity and perfidy cause her to disobey the gods' instructions, and a host of evils is released into the world. Just as YHWH punished Eve for her curiosity and disobedience, Zeus sentences Pandora and all women to be eternally dominated by their fathers and husbands and to suffer in childbirth.[9]

## Goddess Deprivation and the Loss of Balance

With the murder and exile of the Goddess, men attempted to absolve themselves of partnership with the feminine, leading to a contemporary world that is fundamentally lopsided—technologically advanced but spiritually deprived. Scientific research reports that our society's overreliance on the masculine-leaning left brain is a major cause of endemic stress, loneliness, humorlessness, and strained family relationships. Such a conclusion was reported by biofeedback researchers at Princeton University studying our culture's "over-use of left hemispheric or linear information processing skills." They determined that continuous overemphasis on such left-brain processes as analysis, hierarchy, time consciousness, and competitiveness is a major factor in the breakdown of human relationships and a generalized cultural dysfunction.[10]

In Iain McGilchrist's meticulous study of hemispheric function, *The Master and His Emissary: The Divided Brain and the Making of the Western World*, the author puts the matter in even more alarming terms. He characterizes the culturally induced disruption of the synchrony between cerebral hemispheres as a battle, with a dysfunctional left brain effectively waging war against the right brain:

> The left hemisphere, which creates a sort of self-reflexive virtual world, has blocked off the available exits, the ways out of the hall of mirrors, into a reality which the right hemisphere could enable us to understand. . . . An increasingly mechanistic, fragmented, decontextualized world, marked by unwarranted optimism mixed with paranoia and a feeling of emptiness, has come about, reflecting . . . the unopposed action of a dysfunctional left hemisphere.[11]

It is as if the mythic showdown between Marduk vs. Tiamat is going on inside our skulls.

How this ongoing battle plays out in the lives of individuals was brought pointedly to my attention a few years ago by the synchronicity of a chance encounter and a newspaper article. One morning when I was scheduled for a routine medical test at a large hospital in Washington, DC, I took the Metro from my suburban neighborhood into the city. I was able to leave after the prime commuter hour, so the train ride was a welcome interval that allowed me to read that day's *Washington Post*. My attention was caught by a feature article about a Franciscan monastery in the city that had constructed a small hermitage on its grounds as an effort to nurture the spiritual well-being of stressed urbanites. The hermitage was a simple, pleasant space where retreatants could rest, read, or meditate at their own discretion, with no pressure to participate in a set program or keep to a schedule. They were asked only to leave daily distractions behind and turn off their electronic devices for the duration of their stay. But the good intentions of the Franciscans were thwarted from an unexpected source—the internal programming of retreatants. It seemed that even away from the distractions of routine, people found it impossible just to "be." They became so anxious about "doing solitude wrong" that in the absence of structure, they soon found themselves making to-do lists. The article quoted a former Trappist monk and psychologist who observed that for most people silence has become "like trying to make a U-turn at rush hour. We're caught up in the momentum of the perceived urgency of the next thing."[12]

When I reached the hospital, I was ushered to a small, darkened room for the scheduled procedure. Casual chat with the technician and her assistant segued into a serious discussion about the difficulty of pursuing spiritual disciplines in the midst of overly busy lives. Both women confessed that their repeated efforts to pray or meditate were inevitably foiled by the left-brain mental chatter they found it impossible to turn off. Suddenly, I found myself in a sisterhood of three who were living the frustration I had just read about in the article about failed solitude. Our culture had taught each of us to be strivers, constantly reaching for better selves and a better society, yet we found our efforts to nurture ourselves spiritually thwarted because we were caught up in the relentless drive of a civilization that never rests. The whole and balanced state of being we longed for remained out of reach.

Is this state of affairs the only way there is? It is nearly impossible to imagine another way of being than your own if you have never seen anything different. Finding a way out of the *cul-de-sac* McGilchrist describes requires imagining a civilization where the dynamic interplay between masculine and feminine energies is alive and well. To that end, we now turn to the proto-literate culture of the Celts.

## Chapter Seven
# "The Greatest People in Europe"

The Celts were fearless warriors because they wish to inculcate this as one of their leading tenets, that souls do not become extinct, but pass after death from one body to another.

Julius Caesar

We are like dwarfs on the shoulders of giants. We see more things than the ancients and things more distant, but it is due neither to the sharpness of our sight nor the greatness of our stature. It is simply because they have lent us their own."

St Bernard of Clairvaux,<br>on the spirituality of the Celts

Perhaps the best-known literary reference to the Celts occurs in the opening line of Julius Caesar's *Commentary on the Gallic Wars* (first century B.C.E.): "All Gaul is divided into three parts, one of which the Belgae inhabit, the Aquitani another, those who in their own language are called Celts, in ours Gauls, the third." Almost everything we know about the European Celts is from the pens of Greek and Roman writers, and because they considered themselves the only civilized people in the world, much of what they have to say is disparaging. The Classical writers did not hesitate to express their revulsion at certain customs they observed in Celtic warriors, including their table manners, sexual habits, drooping mustaches, and proclivity for taking the severed heads of slain enemies as souvenirs. They also cringed at the warriors' fondness for strong Mediterranean wines drunk full strength instead of diluted with water the way "civilized" men took it. From the perspective of Classical writers, the Celts were uncivilized not only because of their disgusting habits but also because they were illiterate.

## The Barbarians

The mysterious people living in the outback of Europe began to attract the notice of the Mediterranean world around the sixth century B.C.E. Early Greek writers called them "Keltoi," meaning barbarians, or more plainly, "not like us." These Keltoi were seminomadic herdsmen and farmers whose warriors gloried in raiding for treasure. Eventually, their growing numbers threatened Mediterranean civilization. The first sign of the threat they posed was a clash between Celtic warriors and the Romans in 387 B.C.E. The Roman army was caught off guard by a horde of warriors wielding strange weapons and raising an unearthly cacophony as they attacked. Finding themselves overmatched, the Roman soldiers fled for their lives. The Senones warriors then marched to Rome, where they sacked the city and besieged it for seven months. The impasse ended only when the Romans agreed to pay a ransom of one thousand pounds of gold. The invaders had brought their own weights to measure the gold, but when a dispute arose over the weighing, Brennus, the Senones

THE GREATEST PEOPLE IN EUROPE

war chief, threw his sword onto the scales and cried, "Vae victis!"— "Woe to the conquered! " (Livy, *The History of Rome*)

The Celts' effectiveness as warriors galvanized Roman attention. The Classical writers wrote much of the Celts' prowess in fighting. Despite their distaste for the warriors' behavior, they were compelled to acknowledge their worthiness as opponents. They were awed by the Celtic warriors' fearlessness in battle, which they attributed to their belief in reincarnation. The Roman army was quick to adopt elements of Celtic weaponry and battle strategies. The reputation of Celtic warriors caused them to be sought throughout the Mediterranean world as mercenaries and royal bodyguards. In grudging admiration, the Greek geographer Strabo summed up the Celts as courageous, vain, fond of personal ornamentation, and of volatile temperament, "war-mad, high-spirited and quick to battle, but otherwise straightforward and not of evil character." (*Geography* 4.2.2)

While the Classical writers saw the Celts primarily as warriors, the culture was far more complex than that stereotype suggests. These "barbarian" tribes brought a host of innovations and improvements to Europe. Celts built the first roads on the Continent, introduced the wheeled chariot, and initiated numerous improvements in agriculture and animal husbandry. Their skilled metalsmiths produced exquisite jewelry and sophisticated weapons that were prized throughout the known world. Our beloved blue jeans evolved from the trousers the Celts introduced to Europe. Ironically, it was the "filthy barbarians" who introduced the Classical world to the use of soap. Historian Albert Grenier has said that during the two hundred years when they were at the height of their powers, the Celts' seemingly inexhaustible energy and manpower made them "the greatest people in Europe."[1]

Apart from the remarkable fighting abilities of their warriors, the aspect of Celtic culture that most impressed the Classical writers was the advanced learning of their Druids, bards, and seers. Julius Caesar observed that the Druids "have much knowledge of the stars and their motion, of the size of the world and of the earth, of natural philosophy, and of the powers and spheres of action of the immortal gods" (De Bello Gallico, Book 6). The vast learning of the priestly Druid class covered every field from medicine and law to astronomy and natural philosophy. What astounded the Classical world even more was that such advanced learning was attained without the use of scrolls, books, or any form of writing. Celtic education relied entirely on oral methods. If you try to imagine mastering everything from kindergarten all the way through graduate school without the benefit of notes or textbooks, you get an inkling of the staggering accomplishments of the Druids, who spent up to twenty years mastering specialized skills and knowledge. It was beyond belief to Greek and Roman writers that people who didn't write or read, who had neither centralized government nor temples nor libraries nor graven images could retain such depth and breadth of knowledge entirely by oral transmission.

Now we come to the great question: *Why* didn't the Celts avail themselves of literacy? The fact that Druids occasionally borrowed from the Greek, Roman, or Phoenician alphabets to inscribe a name or short message indicates that they were aware of literacy and could have acquired it had they wanted to. Given the overwhelming disadvantages of illiteracy, it's hard to imagine anyone passing up the opportunity to learn to read and write. But the Celts' choice to abstain from literacy wasn't the result of obtuseness or ignorance. It was a spiritual matter.

In the first place, relying on oral transmission was a way of protecting sacred knowledge. Since anything that was written down could be accessed by any reader, refraining from writing protected sacred knowledge from exposure to uninitiated eyes. Lucien Lévy-Bruhl sums up the Celtic attitude: "If the sacred myths were to be divulged, they would be profaned and would thus lose their mystic qualities. Their deeper meaning and efficacy were revealed only to the initiate. Non-initiates regarded them merely as amusements."[2]

The Celts' guarded posture toward literacy also had to do with their belief that sound is a powerful sacred force. Such a belief was not unique to the Celts. The Sanskrit mantra "Nada Brahma" ("the world is sound") expresses the Hindu belief that the universe arises out of sound.[3] The Hebrew Scriptures depict the creative power of sound in YHWH's speaking the world into existence. The scriptures also illustrate the destructive power of sound in the story that a cacophony of trumpets and battle cries caused the walls of Jericho to come tumbling down. Our scientific creation story, the Big Bang Theory, posits that the universe exploded into existence in a long burst of sound. In Irish mythology, the powers of sound are depicted through healing incantations chanted by Druids and the music of magical harps that can soothe, heal, or induce sleep. Irish mythology also boasts that the ancestral deities invented the practice of unnerving the enemy by "shouting and uproar" in battle.

Because so sacred and powerful a force requires careful handling, much of the lengthy training undergone by Druids, bards and seers was devoted to acquiring skills that allowed them to use sound appropriately. A bard's ability to deploy sound effectively is demonstrated in an episode from the Irish *Cath Maige Tuired* ("Second Battle of Moytura," abbreviated *CMT*). As royal bard in the court of Bres the Beautiful, King of the Tuatha de Danaan, the poet Coirpre's duty was to compose poetry in praise of his patron. But should a lord fail to provide his people with the hospitality that was his sacred responsibility, a bard could compose a poetic *satire* ("loss of face") to deprive his patron of dignity or damage his reputation. Despite Bres's impressive qualifications as king, his refusal to provide his people with the feasts and entertainments that were their due made him unfit for his office.

> At that time, Bres held the sovereignty as it had been granted to him. There was great murmuring against him among his maternal kinsmen the Túatha Dé, for their knives were not greased by him. However frequently they might come, their breaths did not smell of ale; and they did not see their poets nor their bards nor their satirists nor their harpers nor their pipers nor their horn-blowers nor their jugglers nor their fools entertaining them in the household.... On one occasion the poet came to the house of Bres seeking hospitality (that is, Coirpre son of Étain, the poet of the Túatha Dé). He entered a narrow, black, dark little house; and there was neither fire nor furniture nor bedding in it. Three small cakes were brought to him on a little dish—and they were dry. The next day he arose, and he was not thankful.

"Not thankful" is a whopping understatement for Coirpre's feelings about Bres's insulting treatment, and anyone who knows how to weaponize sound is a very dangerous person to offend. In retribution for Bres's cheeseparing ways, Coirpre composed what is said to be the first satire in Ireland:

> Without food quickly on a dish,
> Without cow's milk on which a calf grows,
> Without a man's habitation after darkness remains,
> Without paying a company of storytellers
> —let that be Bres's condition.

Coirpre's satire prescribed the withdrawal of the life-sustaining gifts of the feminine: food, milk, shelter, and prosperity. The satire also caused Bres to break out in boils and the land to suffer: "And nought save decay was on Bres from that hour." The power that a bard could wield through his mastery of sound was impressive.

Diodorus Siculus attests that Druids could even use sound to halt armed combat: "For oftentimes as armies approach each other in line of battle with their swords drawn and their spears raised for the charge, these men come forth between them and stop the conflict, as though they had spell-bound some kind of wild animals" (*Biblioteca Historica,* V, 31). If words were potent enough to stop a battle, heal the sick, or bring down a king, there is little wonder that Celts didn't want to risk having them desecrated or stolen by putting them into writing.

## The Celtic Sacred World

The rejection of literacy was only one aspect of Celtic culture that baffled the Greeks and Romans. The Celts were organized into tribal confederations led by chieftains, but they had no cities, no centralized government, no standing army, no coinage, no images of their deities. Julius Caesar judged the Gauls to be profoundly religious, but any temples they built have not survived. We do know that Druid priests presided over religious ceremonies in the natural settings where the earth's spiritual essence was palpable—in groves, on hilltops, or near sacred wells and watercourses. The Continental Celts confounded the Romans by leaving votive offerings of gold and silver unguarded in sacred groves, apparently taking it for granted that no one would dare to touch a sacred offering. Another means by which the Celts offered gifts to the divine realm was by placing them in the waters of streams and wells. This ancient practice is the basis of the legend that King Arthur's sword Excalibur was thrown into a lake, and it survives in our custom of throwing a coin into a fountain while making a wish. It has also yielded a bonanza for modern archaeologists in the form of quantities of precious metals, jewelry, and captured weapons they have recovered from streams and ponds.

Another aspect of Celtic religion that mystified the Classic world was the absence of graven images. An account related by Diodorus Siculus illustrates the Celts' distain for iconic images. In 279 B.C.E., Brennus, king of the Gauls (not the same Brennus who earlier besieged Rome) led his warriors on a treasure raid to the temple of Apollo at the shrine of Delphi. Brennus knew that the Greeks regarded this temple as a most sacred site, so he expected to find there great deposits of gold and silver such as his people offered to their gods. But to his astonishment, the temple held "no dedications of gold or silver," only graven images of the deities. "And when he came only upon images of stone and wood, he laughed at [the Greeks], to think that men, believing that gods have human form, should set up their images in wood and stone." (*The Library of History*, Book 22, 9, 4)

These were the people who challenged Classical Civilization. The fourth century B.C.E. siege of Rome was the opening salvo in an ongoing struggle for supremacy in Europe. Ultimately, the Celts' impressive energy and unparalleled abilities as fighters could not make up for their lack of intertribal cooperation and strategic organization. By the time of Caesar's campaign in Gaul in the first century B.C.E., the power of the Celtic tribes in Europe was on the wane. Gaul fell to the Romans, followed by most of the other Celtic regions. Wherever Rome prevailed, traditional Celtic culture and languages were overwritten by Romanization, and that might have been the end of the Celtic story—except for the existence of Ireland.

# Chapter Eight
# How the Irish Saved
# Celtic Mythology

Christian Ireland preserved, as a legacy from
paganism, the belief in a time when the
supernatural was natural, when the marvelous
was normal.

Marie-Louise Sjoestedt

About the same time Julius Caesar was campaigning
in Gaul, in the first century B.C.E., Agricola, the Gallo-
Roman general responsible for the conquest of much of
Britain, was campaigning in western Scotland. The
historian Tacitus reports that when Agricola's gaze fell upon
Ireland a few miles to the west across a narrow stretch of
the Irish Sea, the general mused that the island could easily
be taken with a single Roman legion. But fortunately for
Celtic culture, the resources of the Roman Empire were
overstretched at the time, and invasion of Ireland was not
a high priority. Agricola was soon recalled to Rome, Ireland
escaped Roman conquest by a hairbreadth, and Celtic oral
tradition lived on in the "island at the edge of the world."

As Roman hegemony encircled the Mediterranean,
Celtic language and culture survived only on the periphery
of the empire. According to St. Jerome, the residents of

Galatia on the easternmost fringe of the empire, still spoke a Celtic language as late as the fourth century C.E. The *Lives* of St. Brigid of Kildare indicate that the Celtic culture established in Ireland in the middle of the first millennium B.C.E. was still flourishing there a thousand years later. Throughout the Celtic fringe of Europe—in Ireland as well as Brittany, Galicia, Cornwall, Wales, the Isle of Man, and Scotland—Celtic language and lore continued to shape local cultures for centuries.

Ireland's geographic isolation made it an ideal refuge for Celtic culture. What has made it possible for us to know anything of that unique culture today was another fortunate circumstance: Christianity brought literacy to Ireland. And while the spread of literacy hastened the demise of Celtic tradition, the Christian missionaries paradoxically wrote down the "pagan superstitions" of the oral culture they worked assiduously to suppress. Such an effort seems a bit like trying to drive a car with one foot on the gas pedal and the other on the brake, but the fact is that we owe the Irish monks a debt of gratitude. Without the work of diligent Irish monastic scribes who transcribed much of the oral tradition, Celtic mythology would have been entirely lost to the world.

### The Scrap Bag

How they went about their work of transcribing the thousands of bits and pieces of stories, songs, genealogies, and legends they inherited from the oral tradition remains a mystery. I imagine all those fragments of oral tradition as being like the contents of old-fashioned scrap bags that were once commonplace in American households. In the days of "waste not, want not," all sorts of fabric remnants from sewing projects and outworn garments were squirreled away against a time when they might come in handy. In the nineteenth century, someone came up with an idea for using those remnants that married thrift with artistry—making crazy quilts. According to an 1884 article in *Harper's Bazaar*, the creation of a crazy quilt could take up to 1,500 hours. The quilts were called "crazy" because of the higgledy-piggledy way swatches of velvet and silk and ribbon were stitched together into blocks. When the blocks were joined together and embellished at the seams with colorful embroidery, this seemingly haphazard array of bits and pieces often became an arresting riot of color and texture. I am the proud caretaker of a beautiful crazy quilt my Great-Aunt Anna conjured from the odds and ends from the family scrap bag in the heyday of the crazy quilt fad.

The work of Irish monastic scribes must have been something like that, pulling tangled remnants of poetry and prose from the great scrap bag of oral tradition and stitching them together into coherent montages. Perhaps their most important assemblage is *Lebor Gabala Erenn* (*LGE*), in which they created coherence by anchoring the Irish oral tradition to a framework of biblical history. *LGE*, which followed the Irish all the way back to Adam and linked them with the Children of Israel, was accepted as conventional history until the nineteenth century.

Two things Ireland lacked posed a challenge for the Church faced in the early centuries of missionizing: The island had neither cities nor a tradition of literacy. In the absence of cities, the Irish Church became anchored in monastic institutions, and the influence traditionally wielded by urban-based diocesan bishops was exercised by their abbesses and abbots. To compensate for the absence of literacy, monasteries created scriptoria and set monks to work producing the literature the church needed. The *Lives* of St. Brigid exemplify the inspirational literature they produced. Thanks to the foresight of some abbesses and abbots, monks also produced transcriptions of oral myths. Ironically, it came to pass that oral myths including the goddess Brigid were being transcribed during the same centuries that works documenting the life of Brigid of Kildare were being produced.

Imagine traveling back in time to seventh-century Ireland to visit a small, unprepossessing collection of rustic huts that house a Christian monastic community. In the hut that serves as a scriptorium, a monk—we'll call him "Brother Dáire"— hunches intently over a desk beside the single window as he carefully forms letters on a sheet of vellum with a quill pen. Dáire is setting down an old song that happens to be part of the repertoire of his uncle, the bard Áed. This is one of Dáire's favorites, although privately he suspects that some of the things in Áed's songs aren't fit subjects for the ears of decent Christians. Still, Dáire's abbot insists that all stories are worth remembering, even pagan stories, and the abbot is a wise man. So, Dáire persists at his labor, hoping to finish the page before the afternoon light fades. Among the deities and heroes who populate the old songs and stories Dáire and scribes like him will record and edit over the next several centuries is a goddess called Brigid.

Now imagine going to another part of Ireland, the Currach Plain, to visit a far more imposing foundation, the renowned Abbey of Kildare. Here in the scriptorium one Brother Cogitosus is beginning the formidable task of creating a biography of the blessed St. Brigid, which he will call *Vita Sanctae Brigitae (Life of St. Brigid)*, or (*VSB*). Cogitosus begins his manuscript humbly, protesting his inadequacy for the task. His talent is mediocre, he says, his memory inadequate, his speech too rustic. He is eager for his efforts to do justice to the reputation of the revered abbess who made Kildare a magnet for "countless people of both sexes drawn by the fame of her good deeds [who] flocked to her from every province throughout the whole of Ireland" (*VSB*, §4). He wants his account of "the greatness and the worth of the virgin radiant with good virtues" to inspire all who read it (*VSB*, §3). Cogitosus can choose from a multitude of legends about the beloved St. Brigid and her miracles handed down "without any shadow of ambiguity by well-informed elders" (*VSB*, §2). In time, this first biography of a saint ever written in Ireland will serve as a model for lives of other saints, including St. Patrick and St. Columba.

Monks like Daire who labored to transcribe the remnants collected in the oral scrap bag faced another challenge. The scribes had to find ways to reconcile the radically dissimilar worldviews of the myths and their own Christian faith. The Christian belief in a hierarchically ordered universe wherein the human and divine realms were separated by a great chasm could hardly have been more unlike the world of Irish myth, where the supernatural permeated human and divine realms separated by permeable boundaries. The fluidity of this world made possible the agreement by which the Milesians and the Tuatha de Danaan shared the island of Ireland, with the Milesians living on the surface and the Danaans dwelling in the Otherworld. The semidivine Danaans retained the ability to appear in the human world while allowing the mortal Milesians to visit Otherworld, located in tumuli, on islands, and under the sea. Such permeability between worlds survives in the belief in "thin places" and "thin times" in which the visible world opens to the invisible.

One technique Christian scribes adopted to preserve the mythic world's unique sense of time and space was to emphasize the discontinuity between the present and the era when "beings lived or events happened such as one no longer sees in our days."[1] Sometimes they explained the fantastic things they recorded as the work of demons. For instance, the tale of a talking sword that is able to recount all the deeds it has done is accompanied by the comment "For the diabolical power was great before the faith, and it was so great that devils used to fight with men in bodily form, and used to show delights and mysteries to them. And people believed that they were immortal."[2] But some scribes found fault with these ways of distancing themselves from the myths they transcribed. One disgruntled copyist noted in the margins of *Táin Bó Cúaligne* ("The Cattle Raid of Cooley"), "But I who have written this history, or rather story, do not give faith to many of the things in this history or story. For some things therein are delusions of the demons, some things are poetic figments, some are like the truth and some are not, and some are for the amusement of fools!"[3]

Despite the scribes' efforts to place the old myths within the doctrinal bounds of the Church, the world of the myths persisted in the consciousness of the Irish. Christian reinterpretation of the myths did not eradicate the people's abiding love for the figures who populated pagan storytelling and song or their ingrained resistance to observing stringent boundaries. Long past the time when Christian monotheism began its gradual displacement of polytheism, the fluid world of heroes and deities identified with natural forces continued to flourish in the Gaelic imagination.

Ireland's oral tradition together with its unique geographic isolation formed a matrix in which feminine energies were able to thrive and collaborate with human imagination long past the time when literacy had suppressed Divine Feminine influence in the Classical world. Ironically, it was the introduction of literacy that made it possible for us to know anything today of Celtic mythology. Literacy was also the tool by which the Irish Church perpetuated its own version of Brigid as part of its campaign to replace traditional beliefs with Christian faith. Ultimately, it was the Gaelic imagination that successfully synthesized literate and ancient oral traditions by producing a Brigid sanctioned by the Church yet deeply connected with her pagan roots.

# PART THREE

# The Return of the Goddess

# &

# The Age of Aquarius

# Chapter Nine
# The Return of the Divine Feminine

Her names are innumerable.
Erich Neumann

I put songs and music on the wind before ever the bells of the chapels were rung in the West or heard in the East. I am Brighid of the Mantle, but I am also Brighid-Conception-of-the-Waves, and Brighid of the Immortal Host, Brighid of the Slim Fairy Folk, Melodious-Mouthed Brighid of the Tribe of the Green Mantles, and I am older than Friday and am as old as Monday. And in the Land of Eternal Youth my name is Mountain Traveller; in the Country of the Waves it is Greyhound; and in the Country of Ancient Years it is Seek-Beyond. And I have been a breath in your heart. And the day has its feet to it that will see me coming into the hearts of men and women like a flame upon dry grass, like a flame of wind in a great wood.

Fiona MacLeod, "The Gaelic Heart"

Early in my journey with Brigid, I was surprised to discover that she has a flourishing following today. Wiccans and neo-Pagans who revere her as a living goddess celebrate her festival of Imbolc and create prayers and rituals in her name. Some environmental activists have adopted her as a patroness. In Kildare, her perpetual sacred flame has been rekindled by an order of Brigidine nuns who tend a sacred well dedicated to Brigid and carry out a ministry of peace-making in her name. Perhaps her most unlikely following in recent years came from supporters of the Irish pro-choice movement, who embraced St. Brigid during a referendum on abortion rights in Ireland. This latter-day "Brigidomania" is accompanied by a deluge of Brigid-focused websites, books, conferences, pilgrimages, and visual art. It seems that the prophecy Fiona MacLeod put in Brigid's mouth, foretelling that she would one day return to "the hearts of men and women," is now being fulfilled.

A resurgence of Divine Feminine energy in our goddess-deprived culture seems a promising sign that our shared reality may be shifting toward a perception of the sacred dance of Yang and Yin. Yet it would be a mistake to expect a quick and painless rebalancing of a Yang-leaning culture that has evolved through such a long time. The Divine Feminine is unlikely to appear like a fairy godmother to banish our problems with a flick of her magic wand. Celtic lore teaches us that the Divine Feminine has many faces and that there is more than one kind of magic wand. The *Brideog* effigy of Imbolc had a white magic wand representing the spring renewal Brigid brought, while her counterpart, the Cailleach, had a *slachdan* that inflicted cold and lifelessness.

The Divine Feminine now arising in our collective awareness includes Brigid's counterpart, the ferocious

Cailleach. The Dark Mother Cailleach is expressing her rage against humanity for centuries of irresponsible stewardship of the Earth and maltreatment of its people. In her hands, the sacred, purifying elements of fire and water are being used to purge the Earth through fiery holocausts raging across many parts of the globe and devastating floods that drown cities and reshape continents. Her wrath can be seen in the COVID-19 pandemic, whereby humanity has been brought to its knees by the unchecked replication of a tiny fragment of DNA, the sacred feminine power of reproduction unbridled.

Dolores Whelan writes of this inescapable aspect of the Divine Feminine:

> The Cailleach is the embodiment of the tough mother-love that challenges her children to stop acting in destructive ways. It is the energy that refuses to indulge in inappropriate personal or societal dreams. It is the energy that will bring death to those dreams and fantasies that are not aligned with our highest good. Yet this Cailleach energy also will support the emergence and manifestation in the world of the highest and deepest within in us. It will hold us safely as we embrace the darkness within ourselves and our society. It is an energy that insists that we stand still, open our hearts, and feel our own pain and the pain of the earth. This is the energy that teaches us how to stay with the process when things are difficult. This energy will not allow us to run away.[1]

Our present circumstances call for the wisdom of balance embodied in the Celtic sovereignty union. Finding our way forward depends on accepting and relating to the dark aspects the Divine Feminine is showing us now. The sovereignty union held the masculine and feminine energies that sustained human society in a dynamic balance. Such a balance could be established neither by strategy nor by sword. It could be achieved only by coming to terms with the most terrifying aspects of the goddess and finding a way to relate to them. Only when the masculine wooed her through vulnerability, humility, and risk did the haglike goddess reveal her benign face. Only then could the relationship move forward.

Access to gifts of the goddess that can lead to a balanced way of being will become available only as we learn to embrace the shadow in ourselves and in our society. Of the Divine Feminine's many attributes, I believe three to be particularly apposite at this juncture. They are:

- Vision: The ability to discern new perspectives
- Liminality: The ability to cultivate patience in transitional times
- *Viriditas:* The ability to renew the abused Earth and the human spirit.

### Divine Feminine Vision

The aftermath of Brigid's rejection of the marriage her family had arranged for her emphasizes eyesight. *Bethu Brigte's* description of the dramatic set-to with her brothers includes self-imposed blindness and exploding eyeballs:

Her brothers were grieved at her depriving them of the bride-price. There were poor people living close to Dubthach's house. She went one day carrying a small load for them. Her brothers, her father's sons, who had come from Mag Lifi, met her. Some of them were laughing at her; others were not pleased with her, namely Bacéne, who said: 'The beautiful eye which is in your head will be betrothed to a man though you like it or not.' Thereupon she immediately thrusts her finger into her eye. 'Here is that beautiful eye for you', said Brigit. 'I deem it unlikely', said she, 'that anyone will ask you for a blind girl.' Her brothers rush about her at once save that there was no water near them to wash the wound. 'Put', said she, 'my staff about this sod in front of you.' That was done. A stream gushed forth from the earth. And she cursed Bacéne and his descendants, and said: 'Soon your two eyes will burst in your head.' And it happened thus (§15).

Imagine the brothers' shock when the sister they were trying to tease and cajole into submission unleashed supernatural powers! The destruction of the physical organ of sight emphasizes both Brigid's determination and the inner vision on which she relied in order to discern the right path for herself.

The inner vision that allows us to find pathways where none existed before is a critical gift in the midst of the pandemic. Daily life is bringing forth remarkable creativity as people improvise new ways of doing the things that must be done. We have no way of knowing how long access to businesses, schools, theaters, restaurants, houses of worship, and all the other places we want to go will be restricted, but it is already clear that the world is being significantly rearranged. Many aspects of life will never return to what we yearningly call "normal."

A few weeks into the initial coronavirus lockdown, some curious phenomena began to appear. People from many parts of the world reported markedly cleaner air and water, and posted on social media photos of wildlife roaming empty city streets. These unexpected benefits to our ecosystem as a result of the extreme measures being adopted for the sake of public health call our old "normality" into question. Many of us are asking if we want to go back to a normality that includes traffic-clogged roadways and industrial wastes spewing into sky and water. Could we find less destructive ways of coexisting with one another and with the planet? Despite the dire economic consequences of the pandemic, this extended pause in business as usual is an unparalleled opportunity to take a deep look at our values and to reenvision our institutions and common enterprises. There will probably never be a better opportunity to take a fresh look at how we do things here on Earth. It's an offer we can't afford to refuse.

### Divine Feminine Liminality

The pandemic reminds us daily how much we hate ambiguity and waiting. Which of us has not fumed when we found ourselves sitting behind the steering wheel at a sluggish red light or standing in a slow-moving line at a checkout counter? The cultural imperative to make every second count, 24 hours a day, seven days a week, 365 days a year can make the most mundane frustrations feel like personal affronts. Our forward-surging culture does not equip us to deal with delay or ambiguity. Without adequate language for talking about in-betweenness, we often resort to judgmental words like "indecisive," "unproductive," or just plain "stuck." Like the hapless retreatants at the Franciscans' urban hermitage, finding ourselves without a plan of action can fill us with anxiety and guilt. Yet, if we can learn to tolerate the discomfort of liminal states, we may be surprised to discover "wasted" intervals to be thresholds that lead to new possibilities.

An episode in the Irish myth of Diarmuid and Gráinne illustrates the feminine gift of finding hidden possibilities within liminal states. Their story begins at the court of Fionn mac Cumhaill, the boy we last met sucking the juices of the Salmon of Wisdom from his thumb, who has grown up to be a famous hunter-warrior and High King of Ireland. A wedding feast is in progress celebrating Fionn's marriage to Gráinne, the daughter of Cormac mac Airt, following the death of his queen. During the festivities, Gráinne notices Diarmud, one of the Fianna, King Fionn's celebrated band of warriors, and her glance happens to fall on the enchanted "love spot" on his forehead, which causes anyone who sees it to fall instantly in love with him. Gráinne is so hopelessly love-struck that she loses all thoughts of marrying the aging king. She slips a sleeping draught into the wine the king and his guests are drinking and demands that Diarmuid elope with her immediately. Diarmuid is torn between love of Gráinne and his sworn loyalty to the king, but he is unwilling to betray either. Unable to take his fate into his own hands, he passes the problem to Gráinne. Diarmuid says he will come with her only if she comes to him neither by day nor by night, neither riding nor walking, neither dressed nor undressed, neither within nor without. With that, he thinks he has solved the problem by creating a set of conditions that get him out of either betraying his king or rejecting Gráinne outright. But at dusk Gráinne appears at the door of his chamber clad in a fairy garment, with one leg over a goat's back and one foot on the ground. On the threshold she announces, "Here I am. I am neither within nor without. I've come neither by day nor by night, neither riding nor walking, neither dressed nor undressed." Diarmuid has not taken into account the feminine genius elicited by liminal situations. Gráinne has met his conditions, so he has no choice but to elope with her.

The poet John Keats made a valuable contribution to our sparse vocabulary of liminality in a letter to his brothers when he called attention to the paradox that the uncomfortable tension of uncertainty may actually be pregnant with possibilities. Keats observed that certain great writers had the unique gift of being able to be "in uncertainties, mysteries, doubts, without any irritable reaching after fact and reason."[2] He called this capacity "negative capability." Perhaps the negative capability Keats identified as a gift of great writers can also be intentionally cultivated by individuals as they grow toward consciousness. Negotiating times of doubt and uncertainty can become a valuable spiritual practice if we can forgo the false certainty of external authorities and accept things *just as they are.* Increasing our toleration for the inescapable liminality of life can help us move forward into the unknown with less anxiety and more confidence, the way an intrepid Brigid once forged ahead across unbroken land toward an undefined future.

### *Viriditas:* Holy Greening Power of the Divine Feminine

Cogitosus's account of Brigid's consecration says that she radiated a renewing force so powerful that even an incidental touch of her hand could restore seasoned wood to verdant life:

> Kneeling humbly before God and the bishop as well as before the altar and offering her virginal crown to almighty God, [Brigid] touched with her hand the wooden base on which the altar rested. And to commemorate her unsullied virtue, this wood flourishes fresh and green to the present day as if it had not been cut down and stripped of its bark but was attached to its roots. And to this day it rids all the faithful of afflictions and disease (*VSB*, § 2).

The Divine Feminine's gift of fructifying and renewing life has often been remarked. Three thousand years ago, Lao-Tzu called "the mysterious feminine . . . the spirit of the fountain [that] never dies" *(I Ching, §6)*. For Dylan Thomas, it was "the force that through the green fuse drives the flower." Science fiction writer Kim Stanley Robinson identifies "the driving force in the cosmos" as a "holy greening power we call *viriditas*."[3] The name *viriditas* Robinson uses to describe the greening power of the Divine Feminine is a portmanteau word created by medieval writers from the Latin words for "green" *(viridis)* and "truth" *(veritas)*.

This "most honored Greening Force [of *viriditas*]. . . enfolded in the weaving of divine mysteries" was a central theme in the mystical writings of Hildegard of Bingen. She saw it as an element of the divine nature embodied in the Virgin Mary, thus it was the feminine aspect of the Divine. Hildegard believed that the *viriditas* that fueled the verdant growth of the vegetables and herbs in her garden was essential to the flourishing of human society, able to heal even the severe social and moral desiccation she observed in twelfth-century Europe:

> Now in the people that were meant to be green
> there is no more life of any kind.
> There is only shriveled barrenness.
> The winds are burdened
> by the utterly awful stink of evil,
> selfish goings-on.
> Thunderstorms menace.
> There pours forth an unnatural,
> a loathsome darkness
> that withers the green
> and wizens the fruit
> that was to serve as food for the people.
> Sometimes this layer of air is full,
> full of a fog that is the source
> of many destructive and barren creatures
> that destroy and damage the earth,
> rendering it incapable of sustaining humanity.
> The earth should not be injured!
> The earth must not be destroyed!"

We in the twenty-first century are no less in need of *viriditas* than were Hildegard's twelfth-century contemporaries. In our own time, environmentalist Joanna Macy's writings resonate with Hildegard's perception of *viriditas* as the force that both empowers the growth of plants and enables humans to heal. Macy sees the greening of the Earth as inextricably linked with a leap forward in consciousness:

The conventional notion of the self with which we have been raised and to which we have been conditioned by mainstream culture is being undermined. What Alan Watts called "the skin-encapsulated ego" and Gregory Bateson referred to as "the epistemological error of mainstream Occidental civilization" is being peeled off. It is being replaced by wider constructs of identity and self-interest, by what philosopher Arne Naess termed the ecological self, co-extensive with other beings and the life of our planet. It is what I like to call "the greening of the self."[4]

The role of the Divine Feminine in this forward leap in consciousness is the subject to which we turn in the final chapter.

# Chapter Ten
# The Aquarian Threshold

The end of the world as we know it is the mystical
theme of the space age.
Joseph Campbell

The present upwelling of feminine energies coincides
with a cosmological event that comes around only about
every 2,000 years, the transition from one astrological age
to the next. Carl Jung's study of astrology led him to
observe that the thresholds between astrological ages or
"aeons" produce certain predictable phenomena. In
particular he called attention to a general psychic instability
and what he called "a changing of the gods."

In the 1950s, Jung became very concerned about the
rash of UFO sightings, which were highly distressing to
the public. He elected to write about these disturbing
phenomena in a context of astrological precession, even
though he realized that doing so risked the opprobrium of
his scientific colleagues:

It is not presumption that drives me, but my
conscience as a psychiatrist that bids me fulfill my
duty and prepare those few who will hear me for
coming events which are in accord with the end
of an era. As we know from ancient Egyptian

history, they are symptoms of psychic changes that always appear at the end of one Platonic month and at the beginning of another. Apparently they are changes in the constellation of psychic dominants, of the archetypes or 'gods' as they used to be called, which bring about, or accompany, long-lasting transformations of the collective psyche. This transformation started in the historical era and left its traces first in the passing of the Aeon of Taurus into Aries, and then of Aries into Pisces, whose beginning coincides with the beginning of Christianity. We are now nearing that great change which may be expected when the spring-point enters Aquarius.[1]

In using words like "Platonic month" and "Aeon," Jung is referring to the 26,000-year cycle by which ancient astronomers measured the phenomenon known as "the precession of the equinoxes." Most people know that an equinox—meaning "equal night" —is the point in the solar year midway between solstices, when days and nights are of equal length. But our species doesn't live long enough for individuals to be able to observe that the months in which equinoxes occur, currently March and September, are not eternally fixed. Instead, these points very gradually move, or "precess." This happens because the Earth isn't exactly a perfect sphere and because it's tilted on its axis. The planet wobbles as it spins, like an old-fashioned toy top, causing the pole to travel a slow, circular path through thirteen major constellations every 26,000 years. The entire circuit is called a "Platonic year." The pole's passage through a single constellation, or a "Platonic month," lasts about

2,150 years, usually rounded off to 2,000 years. Over the course of 26,000 years, the spring point gradually moves through the various constellations.

An odd thing about precession, and the reason transitions between aeons are associated with a "changing of the gods," is that mythic and religious archetypes during a given Platonic month correlate with the symbolism of the constellation the pole is traversing. A familiar example is Christianity's association with the fish symbol of Pisces, the constellation through which the pole has been traveling for the past 2,000 years. In the early years of the Piscean era, adherents to the new Christian faith needed to keep a low profile because of the threat of persecution. They could covertly identify themselves to one another by sketching the outline of a fish in the dirt with the toe of a sandal. The fish was the symbol of the new age and by coincidence, ICHTHYS, the Koine Greek word for "fish," can be spelled from the first letters of the phrase *Iēsous Christos, Theou Yios, Sōtēr* ("Jesus Christ, Son of God, Savior").

Similar correlations emerge in each Platonic month. When the pole was traveling through the sign of Taurus (ca. 4000 B.C.E. to 2000 B.C.E.), for example, the animals used for sacrifices were the bull or calf. When Earth's pole moved from the sign of Taurus to the sign of Aries the Ram, about 2000 B.C.E., the sheep or lamb became the principal animal used in ritual sacrifices. The Hebrew Scriptures, which came into being during the Arian Age, reflect this iconography throughout, with shepherds like David and Abraham being identified as archetypal leaders and the ram's horn being used as the call to ritual observance. Arian iconography still prevailed at the beginning of the Common Era, when Jesus came along, but because Aries was by then transitioning to Pisces, we find the New

Testament Gospels drawing upon iconography from both aeons. Jesus is described with epithets like "Good Shepherd" and "Lamb of God" at the same time he is depicted recruiting fishermen as disciples and feeding multitudes with miraculous multiplications of fish. This overlapping symbolism in Christianity survives to the present day in the liturgical regalia worn by popes and bishops: They carry a shepherd's crook in their hands, while on their heads they wear a miter shaped like the open mouth of a fish.

Now, 2,000 years on, the unrelenting precessional clock has ticked forward, and we find ourselves on the threshold between the Age of Pisces and the Age of Aquarius. Jung's observations about the psychic instability of thresholds between aeons amount to a psychic weather report: "Archetypal transition continuing for the foreseeable future. Expect global weirdness." Along with global weirdness, the threshold between ages is bringing a transition in predominant archetypes, or "changing of the gods," a necessary and inevitable change as humans evolve into higher stages of consciousness. It seems that weirdness and new archetypes are a package deal.

Most of us don't much care for all the upheaval going on in the world right now. On the whole, we'd much rather everything stayed the way we've learned to think of as "normal." Yet upheaval is an inevitable part of the transition. The turmoil and change in dreams and news headlines that scare us senseless are forcing us to relinquish old gods, old institutions, and old ways of thinking in preparation for the emergence of the new.

Some months before the arrival of the COVID-19 pandemic I had dream full of disturbing images:

It is night. I am at home in the house my family lived in when I was an adolescent. A fierce storm is raging outside, but indoors, all is cozy and secure. The aroma of a turkey roasting in the oven pervades the quiet house as I await the arrival of family members for dinner. I am in the kitchen attending to the roast when suddenly the corner of the ceiling collapses in a cascade of lath and plaster. Moments later I am still reeling from this disaster when the bathroom toilet explodes. I wrench open the kitchen door to the outside and find a wet, bedraggled cat eager to come inside. I rush out through the storm and make my way to a nearby church. I am relieved to find other people in the basement, volunteers cleaning up debris from a remodeling project. But as the volunteers go about their work, the storm slams into the upper floors of the church, sending stone rubble and timbers crashing into the basement. The pastor comes to inspect the damage and just shakes his head, having no idea what to do. I join church volunteers who are collecting food and clothing for the people made homeless by the storm. I think perhaps I should go home and get the turkey to share. But before we can act on those plans, the storm worsens, and the church basement becomes uninhabitable. The basement is full of fallen timbers, and there's no longer a working stove or toilet. I realize that our well-intentioned volunteer efforts to help others are fruitless. There is no longer a distinction between victims and helpers. Now all of us are refugees from chaos, simply struggling to survive.

In the dream I'm in the kitchen, the place for preparing nurturing food, waiting for my family, when things start to fall apart. Falling ceilings, exploding pipes, and collapsing buildings in the midst of a violent storm suggest that the structures that once provided protection are crumbling. The dream also portrays a collapse of the hierarchy separating "haves" and "have-nots," as the helpers come to share the status of the ones they were trying to help. Now all of us are "in the same boat" with the millions of refugees we've seen in countless news photographs. We are all refugees from chaos.

We are inclined to interpret terrifying dream images as omens of Armageddon. Unsettling dreams fuel a common apprehension that something terrible is about to terminate our civilization, and possibly all human life on Earth. But Joseph Campbell offers another perspective. Campbell saw the present turbulence not as a series of apocalyptic omens but as hopeful signs of an evolution in human consciousness. Near the end of his life, Campbell said in an interview, "The end of the world as we know it is the mystical theme of the space age." The end of the world *as we know it.*

> The world as the center of the universe, the world divided from the heavens, the world bound by horizons in which love is reserved for members of the in-group: that is the world that is passing away. Apocalypse does not point to a fiery Armageddon but to the fact that our ignorance and our complacency are coming to an end. Our divided, schizophrenic world view, with no mythology adequate to coordinate our conscious and unconscious—that is what is coming to an

end. The exclusivism of there being only one way in which we can be saved, the idea that there is a single religious group that is in sole possession of the truth—that is the world as we know it that must pass away. What is the kingdom? It lies in our realization of the ubiquity of the divine presence in our neighbors, in our enemies, in all of us.[2]

From this perspective, those dreams that wake us in the night with pounding hearts are essential aspects of the preparation for humanity's next developmental task. "The end of the world as we know it" is a wobbly threshold where we are being shaken loose from our dependence on dysfunctional institutions and outworn prejudices that serve neither humanity nor Earth in the long run. Campbell sees this big shake-up as a gift that is urging us to reattune our internal guidance systems. It forces us to withdraw our perceptions of divinity from the external so that we can recognize the divine presence within individual human beings. We are ripe for a new mythology that embodies this shift.

## Emerging Mythology

It is all very well to say that we are due for a changing of the gods, but where does mythology come from? Brigid's evolution suggests that mythology emerges through the psyches of human beings engaged with life in the world. Seeds of the stories and archetypes emerge from the dark fecundity of the collective unconscious through dreams and imagination and grow into mythology according to an inherent pattern language, the way a tree unfolds from a seed.

A hint about this mysterious process comes from analyst Max Zeller's account of a dream he shared with Jung. At the time of the dream, Zeller had been brooding over the discouragingly small impact any single analyst could expect to have in the brief course of a professional lifetime. Then he dreamt:

> A temple of vast dimensions was in the process of being built. As far as I could see-ahead, behind, right and left—there were incredible numbers of people building on gigantic pillars. I, too, was building on a pillar. The whole building process was in its very first beginnings, but the foundation was already there, the rest of the building was starting to go up, and I and many others were working on it.

When Zeller recounted his dream to Jung, he was astonished to learn that Jung was already familiar with the scenario he described. "Yes," Jung agreed, "That is the temple we all build on. We don't know the people because, believe me, they build in India and China and in Russia and all over the world. That is the new religion. You know how long it will take until it is built? About six hundred years." When Zeller asked where he knew this from, Jung said, "From dreams. From other people's dreams and from my own. This new religion will come together as far as we can see."[3]

Six hundred years? Sounds like an impossibly long time unless you're a sequoia tree. On one hand, Jung's assurance that a new religious paradigm is in the works sounds like good news, but that relief is countered by the disheartening realization that no one now living will see it completed, nor for that matter can we do much in the meantime to hurry it along. This liminal period promises to be a lengthy one that will require all the trust in the reliability of universal processes we can muster.

The beach has always been my favorite liminal zone. When I was a child, I spent hours happily lost in the blissful occupation of digging holes in the damp sand. I loved the satisfying "crunch" my little metal spade made as it bit into the sand and the way the sand walls of my little excavation would hold their shape as I dug deeper. Most of all, I loved the mysterious way the hole I had dug would already be filling with up with water from the bottom even before I could fetch a pailful to pour in. For me, that's an image of how myth emerges from the unconscious. It wells up. Even as we mourn the loss of the safety and confidence we once drew from familiar certainties (and here you can name what those were for you), the archetypes that guide the development of human consciousness never cease welling up into the questions of our lives. We can't hurry the process along, but we can depend on it. We need the kind of liminal patience Rilke commends to the young poet who seeks his advice:

> Be patient toward all that is unsolved in your heart and try to love the *questions themselves* . . . Do not now seek the answers, which cannot be given you because you would not be able to live them And the point is, to live everything. Live the questions now. Perhaps you will then gradually, without noticing it, live along some distant day into the answer.[4]

## The Water Bearer and New Mythology

As Aquarius the Water Bearer rises on the horizon, a new set of archetypes to meet the questions in the human heart is welling up in our midst. Aquarius is symbolized by the image of a human figure pouring water from an earthen jar. The ancient Babylonians and Egyptians saw in the stars of Aquarius the god who poured out the waters that flooded the rivers each year. When the ancient Greeks looked up into the night sky, they saw the image of the beautiful youth Ganymede, cupbearer to the Olympian gods, pouring an endless stream of water from his earthen jar. Celtic Christians wove the image of the water bearer into folklore at points where Brigid's story touched stories of Jesus. One Hebridean tale makes Brigid the daughter of the innkeeper who served as the water carrier for the village of Bethlehem. Another story says that when Bride located Jesus by looking through her virtual telescope and went to the well to meet him, she was accompanied by her husband, the man who carried the water with which Jesus washed the feet of his disciples.

An intriguing passage in the Gospel of Luke links Jesus with the sign of the water bearer. Jesus is instructing Peter and John about arrangements for the Passover meal the disciples will share during their last week in Jerusalem. When they ask where they are to make these preparations, he says, "As you enter the city, a man carrying a jar of water will meet you. Follow him to the house that he enters" (Luke 22:10).

This cryptic instruction to follow the water bearer could be seen as a reference to the future evolution of human consciousness. Christian theology has interpreted the Incarnation as the ultimate revelation of the divine to humanity, the once-and- for-all intersection of transcendence and immanence. Yet, this embodiment of transcendent divinity in human flesh might also be seen as a signpost along the way to the ongoing evolution of consciousness. St. Paul's characterization of Christ as the "firstborn of many brothers and sisters" suggests that Jesus was not the only vehicle of the Christ spirit but a prototype for the birth of the Christ within other humans. The image of a human figure carrying the sacred feminine element of water marks the Aquarian age as an era when divine essence is being relocated into individuals, with each one becoming a potential carrier of transcendent divinity.

Zeller's dream of a universal temple under construction reminds us that the mythology expressing that reality is also a work in progress. Yet inklings of that emerging mythology are appearing in the writings of Jungian writers inspired by the rich possibilities of Aquarian imagery. Edward Edinger, in his commentary on Jung's *Aeon*, focuses on the water vessel as the container of authentic consciousness carried by individuals:

> The aeon of Aquarius will generate individual water carriers. The numinous reality of the psyche will no longer be carried by religious communities—the church, the synagogue, or the mosque—but instead it will be carried by conscious individuals. . . . Individuals are to become the incarnating vessels of the Holy Spirit on an ongoing basis.[5]

In *Return of the Goddess,* Edward C. Whitmont evokes metaphors of pregnancy and birth-giving as he observes that the dawning of the new age is bringing to birth each individual's ability to discover the "indwelling source of authentic conscience and spiritual guidance, the divinity within," or what Jung called the Self.[6]

Helen M. Luke weaves together Piscean and Aquarian imagery in her vision of the spiritual revitalization the new age will bring:

> We are passing out of the age of the fishes; they have been drawn up out of the water, but increasingly they have been left to dry up on the shore, despised by men and women who turn to richer and more exciting foods to satisfy their hungers. Nevertheless, if we will contemplate the stars within us, we shall see rising ahead, the image of Aquarius, the water carrier, who stands in the heavens pouring water from a never-failing jar down into the mouth of the stranded fish below him. There can be no better picture of the resurrection for which we wait. The fish is restored to life by a whole man, image of the 'apotheosis of individuality,' who holds consciously in the feminine vessel the living water of the depths.[7]

Such phrases as "conscious individual" and "apotheosis of individuality" in these writings imply a synthesis of masculine and feminine energies. The possibility exists that the dance of Yang and Yin will find new expression through Aquarian mythology. Whitmont imagined some of the radically different social realities that might emerge from a renewed recognition of divine synergy:

> The heroic striving for dominance, conquest, and power, the top-dog-underdog order of things, the

rule of authority and rank, of right and wrong, my way or your way, will have to be modified by the capacity to endure simultaneous, seemingly mutually exclusive opposites. We must learn to appreciate shadings and a spectrum of colors rather than black-and-white systems; to enjoy an intertwining polyphony rather than a single dominant melody to which the rest of the ensemble merely adds harmonizing voices. The new masculine values must respect a variety of different gods or ideals, rather than only one God who is lord and king. Parliamentary cooperation is called for rather than monarchical or even majority rule. Such a value system, far from being chaotic, would initiate a new integrative, moving and balancing order rather than the static version we are used to.[8]

Whitmont and his visionary colleagues are suggesting that the world as we know it is metamorphosing into the world as humans have never known it.

# Epilogue
# Birthing the Divine Self

Perhaps over all there is a great motherhood. . . .
And even in the man there is motherhood, it
seems to me, physical and spiritual; his
procreating is also a kind of giving birth, and
giving birth it is when he creates out of inmost
fullness.
    Rainer Marie Rilke, *Letters to a Young Poet*

If you bring forth what is within you,
what you bring forth will save you.
If you do not bring forth what is within you,
what you do not bring forth will destroy you.
                    *The Gospel of Thomas*

i found god in myself
and i loved her
i loved her fiercely

                    Ntozake Shange

Back there at the holy well in Iona when Brigid first
tapped me on the shoulder, I could not have imagined all
the ways she would come to affect my life, shapeshifting

from muse to psychopomp to BFF. At the moment, though, I must confess that she's trying my patience by manifesting what I would call her "Noodge" persona. Now the girl who once stole things for Jesus and blew off her family by refusing to get married is trying my patience by insisting on having the last word.

Jabbing an elbow into my ribs to make sure I'm paying attention, she wants me to take another look at the Aquarian symbol. "Just look," she demands, "at that earthen jar with water pouring out of it. What do you see?" I answer, eyes rolling, that I see a vessel filled with Divine essence. She waits a beat for the penny to drop. "Oh!" I exclaim, "Now I get it. You mean it could be a pregnant womb." Her satisfied smirk tells me that was the answer she was looking for—but she's not finished yet. With folded arms betraying self-satisfaction, she drives her point home with a question: "And who knows more about birthing a Divine Child than Yours Truly?" Point taken. Brigid means us to understand that she fully intends to go with us into the Age of Aquarius.

In a time when old myths are failing and new ones are still incubating in the womb of the Unconscious, we could ask for no better guide than Brigid. She is Mistress of Thresholds, reminding us that the Divine Feminine thrives in the liminality of the present times. She is Wise Woman, promising that the terrors of our times are not the death throes of humankind but labor pains for what is yet to be born. She is Holy Midwife, assuring those who are ready to accept this promise that she will be present to assist the birth of the Divine Child from each individual.

Even those forward-looking souls who are ready to accept the notion that we are living through a great transformation when the Divine is being relocated into human beings may balk at the image of "spiritual pregnancy." Our culture's long history of masculinity-as-personhood makes many of us shy away from anything that seems too much identified with the feminine, especially something as messy as giving birth. Unless you have yourself borne a child or coached a partner through labor, you may still be influenced by the cartoonish stereotypes of childbirth as a painful and bloody ordeal that takes place behind closed doors and requires lots of hot water. I'm sorry to say that women themselves have perpetuated some of those stereotypes. When I was a girl, women out of the earshot of menfolk often reveled in recitations of "female trouble" and all the woes of pregnancy—morning sickness, stretch marks, and labor pains. Those overheard sessions left me with the impression that childbearing was an opportunity for competitive suffering.

As a woman who has had the privilege of bearing a child, I would like to offer my own testimony that experiencing one's body as a vehicle for the creation of life is a supremely transformative experience. When my turn at childbearing came along, I found it nothing like the ordeal depicted in popular culture or female gossip. Pregnancy felt more like being shanghaied by the Divine Feminine and transported to a different plane of reality. SHE poured into my body and simply took over. SHE redirected my inward workings to knit together all the requisite parts, right down to exquisite little fingernails like tiny, opalescent coquina shells. SHE determined the moment when it was time to push the new creature out of his watery cocoon into the air-breathing world. SHE arranged for my breasts to fill with milk to satisfy his hunger. SHE engendered a fierce love that made me willing to fight a sabretooth tiger barehanded, if necessary, to protect him. I couldn't believe that among all the litanies of delivery room horror stories I had listened to, not a single woman had ever mentioned this amazing aspect of childbirth. I can testify only to my own experience, which was without question the most numinous event in my life.

But having affirmed that giving birth may be a profoundly spiritual experience, let me emphasize that it is not an occasion for solitary heroism. Hebridean women in labor who prayed to Brigid, "Assist thou me, foster mother / The conception to bring from the bone," did not go through their ordeal without the assistance of the knee-wife. Alexander Carmichael relates the story of two young women of St. Kilda who were asked by a visitor to the island why such beauties as they weren't married. They replied, "How can we marry? Has not the knee-wife died?"

During my own pregnancy fifty years ago, I was determined to remain awake and aware during labor and delivery rather than submit to the standard hospital protocol of anesthetized birth, but at the time it was far from easy to arrange. In the end, the cooperation of a sympathetic OB-GYN resident and prenatal coaching from a trained British nurse-midwife made it possible for me to remain relaxed, unanesthetized, and aware for labor and delivery. (The doctor did catch the baby, per hospital regulations.) The midwife could, of course, have delivered the baby had she been permitted to, but what she did provide was a special kind of presence. She knew how the drama of delivery unfolded, along with a thousand variations to the script, so she could tell me what to expect every step of the way. Her tutelage relieved my anxiety and gave me confidence. She convinced me that all I had to do was relax and breathe, singing the little song I had practiced, and let my body do the rest.

Perhaps that positive experience with midwifery accounts for the thrill that went through me many years later when I first learned of the tradition that Brigid had served as midwife to Mary in the stable in Bethlehem. Not one of the typical Nativity scenes crowded with Joseph, shepherds, Magi, angels, and livestock includes anyone who appears capable of offering Mary any practical help. It was truly gratifying to learn that Celtic folk wisdom had filled this gap by the simple expedient of sending Brigid in to help with practical matters like birthing and swaddling.

As human consciousness evolves beyond the mentality of the herd, the collective religious imagination of the Western world continues to be dominated by the shepherd archetype from the Arian Age. Long past the era when herders were iconic figures in the landscape, the pastor of a congregation is still referred to as "the shepherd of the flock," while members of the flock draw comfort from the assurance that "the Lord is my shepherd." The birth of individuality, however, calls for a different kind of guide. The emergence of consciousness within the individual requires a spiritual midwife. Brigid's assistance to Mary in birthing the Christ Child offers a paradigm for spiritual guidance in the Aquarian age.

Margaret Guenther, one of the mothers of the spiritual direction movement, calls a spiritual midwife a "with-man" or "with-woman," a person qualified not by particular professional credentials but by the ability to recognize the sacred process that is unfolding and be fully present with the soul-bearer as it happens. Spiritual midwifery can be provided by spiritual directors, pastoral counselors, depth psychologists, or *anamchairde* (Gaelic for "soul friends") who are attentive listeners. The spiritual midwife can help the individual understand that giving birth to one's soul is not a problem to be solved but a process to be honored. By the gift of presence, a spiritual midwife affirms a faith that consciousness is part of a great, unfolding process, and that the process can be trusted. Perhaps the most important thing that he or she can offer is the kind of assurance Brigid might have given the frightened, teenaged Mary: "Don't be afraid. All will be well."

Perhaps such an assurance may stand as Brigid's last word to us. This book began with the parabolic story of Brigid's willingness to go boldly into uncharted territory because she believed that something of great worth lay beyond the hazards of the unmarked way. Her audacity had a marvelous side effect; as she crossed the trackless terrain, her footsteps left behind a straight bridge. In our own time, when the uncertain way appears filled with unknown hazards, Brigid's footsteps remind us that we can trust ourselves, and we can trust the journey into the future. The only way to create our own bridges to the future is to put one foot in front of the other, even if we are very afraid.

"Don't be afraid. All will be well." May it be so.

# Notes

## Introduction

[1] *The Tao of Physics: An Exploration of the Parallels between Modern Physics and Eastern Mysticism,* Boulder, CO: Shambala, 1975, 20.
[2] *The Masks of God,* Viking, 1959, Vol. I, 12.

## Chapter Two

[1] *The Archetypes and the Collective Unconscious,* 2nd ed., CW Vol. 9, Princeton Bollingen, 1969, 81.
[2] Carl McColman, *366 Celt: A Year and a Day of Celtic Wisdom and Lore,* Element, 2005, 9.
[3] Celtic Literature Collective, https://www.ancienttexts.org/library/celtic/ctexts/eochaid.html. (page discontinued)
[4] Mary Claire Randolph, "Celtic Smiths and Satirists: Partners in Sorcery," *ELH* 8, no. 3 (1941), 194.
[5] Dáithí Ó hÓgáin, *Myth, Legend, and Romance: An Encyclopedia of the Irish Folk Tradition.* Prentice Hall, 1991, 43-45.
[6] Patricia Monaghan, *Encyclopedia of Celtic Mythology and Folklore,* Checkmark Books, 2008, 420.
[7] Patrick K. Ford, "The Well of Nechtan and 'La Gloire Lumineuse,'" in *Myth in Indo-European Antiquity,* ed. Gerald James Lawson, Los Angeles: University of California Press, 1974.
[8] Sharon Paice MacLeod, *Celtic Myth and Religion,* McFarland, 2011, 37.

## Chapter Three

[1] *Symbols of Plenty,* Canterbury Press, 2006, 6-7.

## Chapter Four

[1] *Carmina Gadelica (Charms of the Gaels: Hymns and Incantations),* Floris Books, 1994, §70n., p. 586. [To facilitate references to other versions of *Carmina Gadelica* (CG) in print and online, original verses and stories are noted with the symbol §. Material from Carmichael's notes is noted with "n" added to the item number.]

## Chapter Five

[1] Séamas Ó Catháin, "The Festival of Brigid the Holy Woman," *Celtica 23 (1999),* 237.
[2] *The Silence of Amor and Where the Forest Murmurs,* Heineman, 1912, 137-38.
[3] Robert Harris, "Rabharta na Feile Bride," Roaringwater Journal. https://roaringwaterjournal.com/tag/rahhharta-na-feile-bride/. (page discontinued)
[4] Ó Catháin, 238.
[5] Ó Catháin, 235.
[6] Ó Catháin, 235.
[7] Brian Wright, *Brigid: Goddess, Druidess and Saint,* The History Press, 2009, 105.
[8] Ó Catháin, 248.
[9] Wright, 119.
[10] Wright, 250.
[11] *The New Yorker,* April 17, 1989, 35.

## Chapter Six

[1] Leonard Shlain, *The Alphabet Versus the Goddess: The Conflict Between Word and Image,* Viking, 1998, 49-50.
[2] Shlain, 48.
[3] *Dancing in the Flames: The Dark Goddess in the Transformation of Consciousness,* Shambhala, 1996, 21.
[4] Georges Charbonnier, *Conversations with Claude Lévi-Strauss,* Jonathan Cape, 1961, 29-30.
[5] Robert Logan, *The Alphabet Effect,* William Morrow, 1986, 72.
[6] Shlain, 83.

[7] Shlain, 121.

[8] Shlain, 121-22.

[9] Shlain, 128-29.

[10] Lester G. Fehmi and George Fritz, "Open Focus: The Attentional Foundation of Health and Well-Being," *Somatics*, Spring (1980), 24-30.

[11] Iain McGilchrist, *The Master and His Emissary: The Divided Brain and the Making of the Western World*, Yale University Press, 2019, 6.

[12] Michelle Boorstein, "Refuge in Silence," *The Washington Post*, December 13, 2012, C1, C9.

## Chapter Seven

[1] Albert Grenier, *Les Gaulles*, Payot, 1945.

[2] Lucien Levy-Bruhl, *La Mentalite Primitive*, 3, cited in Marie-Louise Sjoestedt, *Celtic Gods and Heroes*, Dover Publication, 2002.

[3] Joachim Ernst Berendt, *The World Is Sound: Nada Brahma: Music and the Landscape of Consciousness*, Destiny Books, 1991, 15.

## Chapter Eight

[1] Lucien Levy-Bruhl, 3.

[2] R. I. Best and Osborn Bergin, *Lebor na Huidre*, Dublin, 1929, 4034, cited in Sjoested, 2-3.

[3] Alwyn Rees and Brinley Rees, *Celtic Heritage: Ancient Tradition in Ireland and Wales*, Thames and Hudson, 1961, 24.

## Chapter Nine

[1] "Brigit: Cailleach and Midwife to a New World," in *Brigid: Sun of Womanhood*, ed. Patricia Monaghan and Michael McDermott, Las Vegas, NV: Goddess Ink, 2013, 115.

[2] *The Complete Poetical Works and Letters of John Keats*, Houghton Mifflin, 1899, 277.

[3] Green Mars, Spectra, 1994, 19.

[4] "The Greening of the Self" in *Dharma Gaia*, Alan Hunt-Badiner, ed., Parallax, 1990, 53.

## Chapter Ten

1 *Flying Saucers: A Modern Myth of Things Seen in the Skies (CW X),* *1958,* 589.

2 *Thou Art That: Transforming Religious Metaphor,* New World Library, 2001, 207.

3 *The Dream: The Vision of the Night,* The Analytical Psychology Club of Los Angeles, 1975, 2.

4 *Letters to a Young Poet,* Norton, 1934, 27.

5 *The Aion Lectures: Exploring the Self in C. G. Jung's Aion,* ed. Deborah A. Wesley, Inner City Books, 1996, 193.

6 Edward C. Whitmont, *Return of the Goddess,* Crossroad, 198, x.

7 *Woman, Earth and Spirit: The Feminine in Symbol and Myth,* Crossroad, 1984, 38.

8 Whitmont, 191.

# Bibliography

Aldhouse-Green, Miranda J. *Celtic Goddesses: Warriors, Virgins, and Mothers*. 1st ed. New York: G. Braziller, 1996.

_____. *The World of the Druids*. New York: Thames & Hudson, 1997.

Berendt, Joachim Ernst. *The World Is Sound: Nada Brahma: Music and the Landscape of Consciousness*. Rochester, VT: Destiny Books, 1991.

Bidgood, Ruth. *Symbols of Plenty: Selected Longer Poems*. Norwich, UK: Canterbury Press, 2006.

Boorstein, Michelle. "Refuge in Silence." *The Washington Post*, December 13, 2012.

Brenneman, Walter L. "The Circle and the Cross: Reflections on the Holy Wells of Ireland." *Natural Resources Journal* 45, no. 4, Fall (2005): 789–805.

Campbell, Joseph. *Transformations of Myth through Time*, 1st ed. New York: Perennial Library, 1990.

Campbell, Joseph, and Bill D. Moyers. *The Power of Myth*, 1st ed. New York: Doubleday, 1988.

Capra, Fritjof. *The Tao of Physics: An Exploration of the Parallels between Modern Physics and Eastern Mysticism.* Boulder, CO: Shambhala, 1975.

Carmichael, Alexander. *Carmina Gadelica: Charms of the Gaels: Hymns and Incantations.* Edinburgh, UK: Floris Books, 1992.

Connolly, Seán. "Vita Prima Sanctae Brigitae Background and Historical Value." *The Journal of the Royal Society of Antiquaries of Ireland* 119 (1989): 5–49.

Connolly, Sean, and J.-M. Picard. "Cogitosus's 'Life of St Brigit' Content and Value." *The Journal of the Royal Society of Antiquaries of Ireland* 117 (1987): 5–27.

Cowan, Thomas Dale. *Fire in the Head: Shamanism and the Celtic Spirit,* 1st ed. San Francisco: HarperSan-Francisco, 1993.

Cunliffe, Barry W. *The Ancient Celts.* Oxford; New York: Oxford University Press, 1997.

De Waal, Esther. *The Celtic Way of Prayer.* New York: Image Books, 1999.

Dillon, Myles, and Nora K. Chadwick. *The Celtic Realms.* New York: Barnes & Noble Books, 2003.

Edinger, Edward F. *The Aion Lectures: Exploring the Self in C.G. Jung's Aion.* Ed. Deborah A. Wesley. Toronto, Canada: Inner City Books, 1996.

Fehmi, Lester G and George Fritz. "Open Focus: The Attentional Foundation of Health and Well-Being." *Somatics,* Spring (1980), 24-30.

Ford, Patrick K. "The Well of Nechtan and 'La Gloire Lumineuse.'" In *Myth in Indo-European Antiquity,* ed. Gerald James Lawson. Los Angeles: University of California Press, 1974.

Frazer, James George. *The Golden Bough: A Study in Magic and Religion.* New York: MacMillan Publishing Company, 1922.

Graves, Robert. *The White Goddess: A Historical Grammar of Poetic Myth.* New York: Noonday Press, 2000.

Graves, Robert, and Raphael Patai. *Hebrew Myths: The Book of Genesis.* New York: Greenwich House : Distributed by Crown Publishers, 1983.

Gregory, Augusta. *Irish Myths and Legends.* 1910. Reprint, Philadelphia: Courage Books, 1998.

Grenier, Albert. *Les Gaulles.* Paris: Payot, 1945.

Harris, Robert. "Rabharta na Féile Bríde," *Roaringwater Journal* (website), updated January 31, 2016, https://roaringwaterjournal.com/tag/rabharta-na-feile-bride/. (page discontinued)

Jestice, Phyllis G. *Encyclopedia of Irish Spirituality.* Santa Barbara, CA: ABC-CLIO, 2000.

Jung, C. G., ed. *The I Ching: Or Book of Changes.* Trans. Richard Wilhelm and Cary F. Baynes. 3rd edition. Bollingen Series 19. Princeton, NJ: Princeton University Press, 1967.

_____. *The Archetypes and the Collective Unconscious.* Translated by R. F. C. Hull. 2nd ed. Princeton/ Bollingen Paperbacks 20. Princeton, NJ: Princeton University Press, 1980.

Keats, John. *The Complete Poetical Works and Letters of John Keats, Cambridge Edition.* New York: Houghton Mifflin, 1899.

Livingstone, Sheila. *Scottish Customs.* Edinburgh, UK: Birlinn, 2000.

Luke, Helen M. *Woman, Earth and Spirit: The Feminine in Symbol and Myth.* New York: Crossroad, 1993.

MacCana, Proinsias. *Celtic Mythology.* London: Hamlyn, 1970.

Mackenzie, Donald Alexander. *Wonder Tales from Scottish Myth and Legend.* New York: Frederick A Stokes, 1917.

MacLeod, Fiona. *The Silence of Armor and Where the Forest Murmurs.* London: Heinemann, 1912.

_____. *The Winged Destiny,* New York: Duffield, 1911.

MacLeod, Sharon Plaice. *Celtic Myth and Religion.* Jefferson, NC: McFarland & Co, 2011.

_____. *Celtic Cosmology and the Otherworld: Mythic Origins, Sovereignty, and Liminality.* Jefferson, NC: McFarland and Co., 2018.

Mallory, J. P. *The Origins of the Irish.* New York: Thames & Hudson, 2017.

Mark, Joshua J. "Cuneiform." In *Ancient History Encyclopedia.* Last modified March 15, 2018. https://www.ancient.eu/cuneiform/.

Markale, Jean. *The Celts: Uncovering the Mythic and Historic Origins of Western Culture.* 1st U.S. ed. Rochester, VT: Inner Traditions, 1993.

McGilchrist, Iain. *The Master and His Emissary: The Divided Brain and the Making of the Western World.* New Haven: Yale University Press, 2019.

McNeill, F Marian. *An Iona Anthology.* 3rd ed. 1947. Reprint, Edinburgh, UK: Albyn Press, 1971.

Meyer, Marvin W., editor. *The Nag Hammadi Scriptures: The International Edition.* HarperCollins paperback ed. New York: HarperOne, 2008.

Molloy, Dara. *The Globalisation of God: Celtic Christianity's Nemesis.* Mainistir, Inis Mór, Co. Galway, Ireland: Aisling Publications, 2009.

Monaghan, Patricia. *The Encyclopedia of Celtic Mythology and Folklore*. New York: Infobase Pub., 2008.

_____. *The Red-Haired Girl from the Bog: The Landscape of Celtic Myth and Spirit*. New World Library: Novato, CA, 2004.

Monaghan, Patricia, and Michael McDermott, eds. *Brigit: Sun of Womanhood*. Las Vegas, NV: Goddess Ink, 2013.

Neumann, Erich. *The Great Mother: An Analysis of the Archetype*. Edited by Ralph Manheim. Princeton, NJ: Princeton University Press, 1992.

Ó Catháin, Séamas. "The Festival of Brigit the Holy Woman." *Celtica* 23 (1999): 231–60.

O'Connor, Peter. *Beyond the Mist: What Irish Mythology Can Teach Us About Ourselves*. London: Gollancz, 2000.

Randolph, Mary Claire. "Celtic Smiths and Satirists: Partners in Sorcery." *ELH* 8, no. 3 (1941): 184-97.

Rees, Alwyn D., and B. R. Rees. *Celtic Heritage: Ancient Tradition in Ireland and Wales*. London: Thames and Hudson, 1973.

Shlain, Leonard. *The Alphabet Versus the Goddess: The Conflict Between Word and Image*. New York: Viking, 1998.

Sjoestedt, Marie-Louise. *Celtic Gods and Heroes*. Mineola, NY: Dover Publications, 2000.

Spar, Ira. "Mesopotamian Creation Myth." Heilbrunn Timeline of Art History. Metropolitan Museum of Art, April 2009. http://www.metmuseum.org/toah/hd/epic/hd_epic.htm.

Weatherstone, Lunaea. *Tending Brigid's Flame: Awaken to the Celtic Goddess of the Hearth, Temple, and Forge.* Woodbury, MN: Llewellyn Worldwide, 2015.

Weber, Courtney. *Brigid: History, Mystery, and Magick of the Celtic Goddess,* Weiser Books, San Francisco, 2015.

Whitmont, Edward C. *Return of the Goddess.* New York: Crossroad, 1992.

Wolf, Casey June, and Antone Minard. "The Mythical Pairings of Brig and Bres: Its Origins and Meaning in Cath Maige Tuired." HUM 332 *Celtic Mythology,* September 2015.

Woodman, Marion and Elinor Dickson. *Dancing in the Flames: The Dark Goddess in the Transformation of Consciousness.* Boston: Shambhala, 1996.

Wright, Brian. *Brigid: Goddess, Druidess, and Saint.* Stroud, Gloucestershire, UK: History Press, 2009.

Zeller, Max. *The Dream: The Vision of the Night,* Los Angeles: The Analytical Psychology Club of Los Angeles, 1975.